Dec. 26, 1984

To M&M -

Best regards & thanks for being able to spend part of the holiday season w/ you -

[signature]

STATISTICAL ABSTRACT OF THE UNITED STATES-MEXICO BORDERLANDS

Statistical Abstract of Latin America Supplement Series
Supplement 9
James W. Wilkie, *Series Editor*

INTERNATIONAL ADVISORY BOARD

Dauril Alden, *University of Washington*
Oscar Altimir, *Economic Commission for Latin America, Santiago, Chile*
Jorge Balán, *Centro de Estudios de Estado y Sociedad, Buenos Aires*
Marcelo Carmagnani, *Università di Torino*
Bruce H. Herrick, *Washington and Lee University*
Herbert S. Klein, *Columbia University*
John V. Lombardi, *Indiana University*

William Paul McGreevey, *World Bank*
Markos Mamalakis, *University of Wisconsin–Milwaukee*
Hans Jürgen Puhle, *Universität Bielefeld*
Clark W. Reynolds, *Stanford University*
Peter H. Smith, *Massachusetts Institute of Technology*
Barbara A. Tenenbaum, *University of South Carolina*
John J. TePaske, *Duke University*

EDITORIAL STAFF

Editor: Peter L. Reich
Production coordinator: Colleen H. Trujillo
Editorial analyst: Waldo W. Wilkie
Researcher: Juan Salcedo
Contributors: Mike Farrell, Jerry R. Ladman, Martin E. Rosenfeldt, Kenneth L. Shellhammer

UCLA LATIN AMERICAN CENTER
STATISTICAL AND COMPUTER SUPPORT COMMITTEE

Robert N. Burr, *History*
Sebastián Edwards, *Economics*
David K. Eiteman, *Management*
Edward Gonzalez, *Political Science*
Stephen Haber, *History*
Sergio Melnick, *Urban Planning*

Peter Reich, *History*
Susan Schroeder, *History*
Susan C. M. Scrimshaw, *Public Health*
Edna Monzón de Wilkie, *Latin American Center*

STATISTICAL ABSTRACT of the UNITED STATES- MEXICO BORDERLANDS

PETER L. REICH
Editor

UCLA Latin American Center Publications
University of California, Los Angeles
Los Angeles, California

UCLA Latin American Center Publications
University of California
Los Angeles, California 90024

© 1984 by The Regents of the University of California
All rights reserved
Printed in the United States of America

Library of Congress Cataloging in Publication Data
Main entry under title:

Statistical abstract of the United States-Mexico borderlands.

   (Statistical abstract of Latin America, supplement
series ; suppl. 9)
   1. Mexican-American Border Region--Statistics.
2. Mexican-American Border Region--Economic conditions--
Addresses, essays, lectures. I. Reich, Peter L.,
1955-   . II. Series.
HA218.S72   1984   317.21   83-24922
ISBN 0-87903-243-X

Contents

Tables vi

Explanation of Terms ix

Map of the United States-Mexico Borderlands x

Preface xiii

PART ONE   STATISTICAL TIME SERIES

1. Demography 3
2. Vital Statistics 11
3. Religion 29
4. Immigration 33
5. Employment, Wages, and Prices 41
6. Maquiladoras 51
7. Transportation and Communication 59
8. Agricultural and Fisheries Production 67
9. Mexican-U.S. Economic Relations 73
10. Tourism 79

PART TWO   DEVELOPMENT OF DATA

11. The Economy of Baja California, by Mike Farrell 87
12. The Gap between Theoretical Modeling and the Application of These Models to the U.S.-Mexican Border Economy, by Jerry R. Ladman 101
13. Industrial Technology Transfer for Borderlands Development: The Need for a U.S.-Mexican Data Base, by Martin E. Rosenfeldt 105
14. United States-Mexico Border Economic Interdependence: Input-Output Model Perspectives of the Effects of the 1982 Peso Devaluations on the San Diego Economy, by Kenneth L. Shellhammer 115

Contributors 121

Tables

Detailed data in tables may not equal totals because of rounding.

PART ONE   STATISTICAL TIME SERIES

Chapter 1   Demography
- 100   State Population Census Series, 10 SC, 1900–80
- 101   State Percentages of Border and National Population, 10 SC, 1900–80
- 102   Population Density, 10 SC, 1900–80
- 103   State Population Projections, 10 SC, 1970–2000
- 104   Twin City Populations, 1900–70
- 105   Mexico Border City Population, by State of Origin, 32 SC, 1970
- 106   Persons of Mexican Origin or Descent in the United States, 4 SC, 1970 and 1980

Chapter 2   Vital Statistics
- 200   Births, by State, 10 SC, 1930–81
- 201   Birth Rate, by State, 10 SC, 1930–81
- 202   Births in the United States by Mexican Origin of Parents, 2 SC, 1979
- 203   Deaths, by State, 10 SC, 1930–81
- 204   Marriages, by State, 10 SC, 1930–81
- 205   Divorces, by State, 10 SC, 1930–81

Chapter 3   Religion
- 300   Mexican Population, by Religion, 6 SC, 1900–70
- 301   Mexican Population without Religious Affiliation, 6 SC, 1900–70
- 302   U.S. Catholic Population, 4 SC, 1960–80
- 303   U.S. Jewish Population, 4 SC, 1960–80

Chapter 4   Immigration
- 400   Mexican Immigration to the United States, 1930–79
- 401   U.S. Immigration to Mexico, 1930–73
- 402   Mexican Workers Departing to and Returning from the United States, 6 SC, 1942–67
- 403   Undocumented Mexican Workers in the United States, 1970–81
- 404   U.S. Immigration and Naturalization Service Man-Hours Per Deportable Undocumenteds Located, 1978–82
- 405   Mexican Undocumenteds Counted in the 1980 U.S. Census, by Period of Entry, 1960–80

Chapter 5   Employment, Wages, and Prices
- 500   Economically Active Population, Employment, and Unemployment in Mexican Border Cities, 1960–70
- 501   Economically Active Population in Mexican Border Cities, by Sector, 1970 and 1975
- 502   Employment in U.S. Border Counties, by Sector, 4 SC, 1969 and 1976
- 503   Hispanic Origin Workers in the United States: Civilian Labor Force, Employment, and Unemployment, 5 SC, 1979–80
- 504   Hispanic Origin Workers in the United States: Unemployment Rate, 5 SC, 1976–82
- 505   U.S. Unemployment Rate, 4 SC, 1970–82

506 Daily Minimum Wages in Mexican Border Cities, 1970–81
507 Consumer Price Index for Mexican Border Cities, 1970–80

Chapter 6 Maquiladoras
600 Maquiladora Characteristics, by State and Municipality, 5 SC, 1970–80
601 Maquiladora Characteristics, by Type of Economic Activity, 1974–79
602 Personnel Employed in Maquiladora Industry, by State and Municipality, 5 SC, 1974–80
603 Personnel Employed in Maquiladora Industry, by Type of Economic Activity, 1974–79

Chapter 7 Transportation and Communication
700 Length of Roads, 10 SC, 1960–80
701 Motor Vehicles Registered, 10 SC, 1960–80
702 Airports, 10 SC, 1964–81
703 Telephones in Use, 10 SC, 1960–81
704 Films Shown in Mexico, by National Origin, 6 SC, 1966–80

Chapter 8 Agricultural and Fisheries Production
800 Corn Production, 8 SC, 1975–80
801 Cotton Production, 9 SC, 1975–80
802 Wheat Production, 10 SC, 1975–80
803 Fisheries Production, 7 SC, 1960–80

Chapter 9 Mexican-U.S. Economic Relations
900 Peso-Dollar Exchange Rate, 1930–82
901 Peso-Dollar Exchange Rate, January–December, 1982
902 Mexican-U.S. Trade Totals, 1900–80
903 U.S. Government Grants and Credits to Mexico, 1945–80

Chapter 10 Tourism
1000 Border Tourists, by State and Port of Entry, 5 SC, 1971–79
1001 Tourism and Border Transactions: Mexican Revenue and Expenditures, 1970–80
1002 U.S. Tourists in Mexico, by U.S. State of Departure, 4 SC, 1932–73

PART TWO   DEVELOPMENT OF DATA

Chapter 11 The Economy of Baja California, by Mike Farrell
1100 Baja California Urban and Rural Population, 1930–70
1101 Baja California Share of Production in GDP, 1965 and 1969
1102 Shares of Production Sectors in GDP at Factor Cost, Fifty-Seven Countries Grouped by 1958 GDP per Capita, About 1958
1103 Shares of Production Sectors in Labor Force, Fifty-Nine Countries Grouped by 1958 GDP per Capita, About 1960, and Baja California (BC), 1969
1104 Sectoral Product per Worker and Related Measures at Benchmark Values of GDP per Capita, about 1960, and Baja California, 1969
1105 Male and Female Labor Force Participation Rates by Age Groups, Mexico and Baja California (BC), 1970
1106 Composition of International Trade, 1965 and 1969
1107 Housing Characteristics, Mexico and Baja California, 1970
1108 Distribution of Monthly Income Among the Employed Population, Mexico and Baja California, 1970
1109 Deportable Mexican Nationals Located in California, 1970–76

Chapter 13 Industrial Technology Transfer for Borderlands Development: The Need for a U.S.–Mexican Data Base, by Martin E. Rosenfeldt

1300   Reynosa/McAllen SMSA Co-Variate Analysis: Summary of Economic Indicator Growth Rates, 1970 and 1975
1301   Reynosa/McAllen SMSA Co-Variate Analysis, 1970 and 1975: Cross-Regional Co-Variates in Terms of Comparative Percentages
1302   Reynosa/McAllen SMSA Co-Variate Analysis, 1970 and 1975: Per Capita Value Added by Manufacturing
1303   Reynosa/McAllen SMSA Co-Variate Analysis, 1970 and 1975: Per Capita Growth Rate of GDP in Manufacturing

Chapter 14 United States–Mexico Border Economic Interdependence: Input-Output Model Perspectives of the Effects of the 1982 Peso Devaluations on the San Diego Economy, by Kenneth L. Shellhammer

1400   Estimated Trade and Changes in Trade between Mexico and San Diego, 1982
1401   Direct, Indirect, and Induced Effects of Trade between Mexico and San Diego, 1982, Baseline Estimates (No Devaluation)
1402   Economic Impact of the Mexican Peso Devaluation on San Diego, 1982, Low-Range Estimates (With Devaluation)
1403   Economic Impact of the Mexican Peso Devaluation on San Diego, 1982, High-Range Estimates (With Devaluation)

Explanation of Terms

Symbols

‡   Preliminary, provisional, or unofficial
\#   Zero or negligible (less than half of unit employed, e.g., less than .5 or 500,000)
     Data not available
--   Source does not specify whether data are recorded separately, not applicable, zero or negligible
†   Estimate by or in source

Abbreviations

EAP	economically active population
Ha.	hectare(s)
km, km²	kilometer, square kilometers
M	million (i.e., 000,000 omitted)
MET	metric tons
N	number
S	Borderlands states (U.S.: California, New Mexico, Arizona, Texas; Mexico: Baja California Norte, Sonora, Chihuahua, Coahuila, Nuevo León, Tamaulipas)
SC	Borderlands states, and comparison with Border totals (Mexico and U.S.), and National totals (Mexico and U.S.)
T	thousand
U	unit
US	U.S. currency

Sources

Sources frequently cited. Others accompany individual tables.

AEM	Mexico, Dirección General de Estadística, *Anuario estadístico*
BM-MSD	Banco de México, *Mexico Statistical Data, 1970–1980* (México, D.F., 1981)
CGP	Mexico, Dirección General de Estadística, *Censo general de población*
CP	U.S. Bureau of the Census, *Census of Population*
EIME	Mexico, Secretaría de Programación y Presupuesto, *Estadística de la industria maquiladora de exportación, 1974–1980* (México, D.F., 1981)
HSUS	U.S. Bureau of the Census, *Historical Statistics of the United States*
INS-AR	U.S. Immigration and Naturalization Service, *Annual Report*
LFN	Mexico, Secretaría de Industria y Comercio, *La frontera norte: diagnóstico y perspectivas* (México, D.F., 1975)
MVSR	U.S. Department of Health and Human Services, *Monthly Vital Statistics Report*
SAUS	U.S. Bureau of the Census, *Statistical Abstract of the United States*
USDA-CP	U.S. Department of Agriculture, *Crop Production*
VSSR	U.S. Bureau of the Census, *Vital Statistics—Special Reports*
VSUS	U.S. Public Health Service, *Vital Statistics of the United States*

Weights and Measures

Length	1 kilometer	.6213712 mile
	1.609344 kilometers	1 mile
Area	1 Hectare	2.471054 acres
	.4046856 hectares	1 acre
	1 square kilometer	.3861022 square mile
	2.589988 square kilometers	1 square mile
Weight	1 metric ton	1.1023113 short tons
		.9842065 long ton
	.9071847 metric ton	1 short ton (2,000 lbs)
	1.0160469 metric tons	1 long ton (2,240 pounds)

Agricultural products		Bales per metric ton
Wheat	Bushel (60 lbs)	36.744
Corn	Bushel (56 lbs)	39.638
Cotton	Gross Bales (500 lbs)	4.409
	Net Bales (480 lbs)	4.593

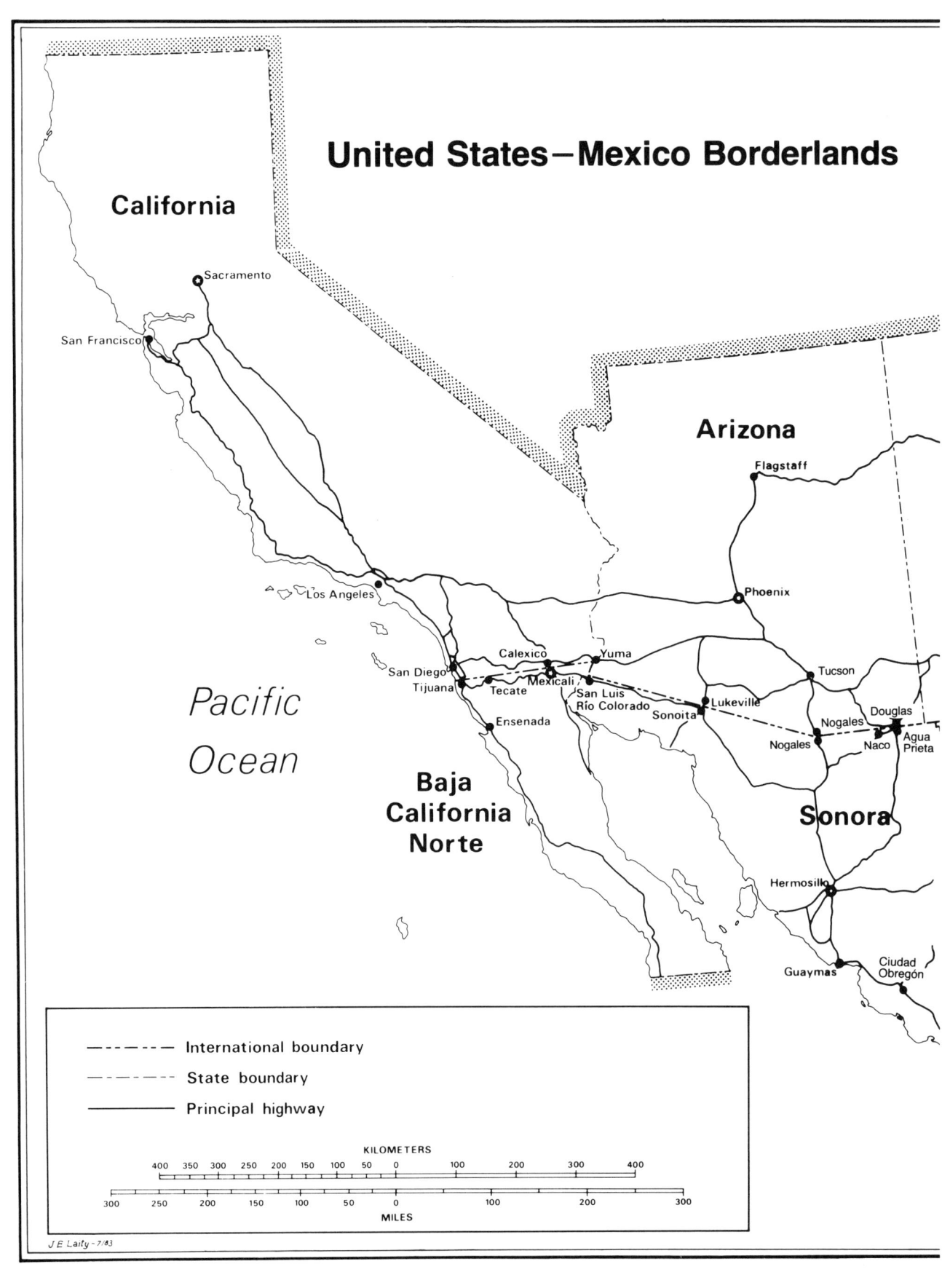

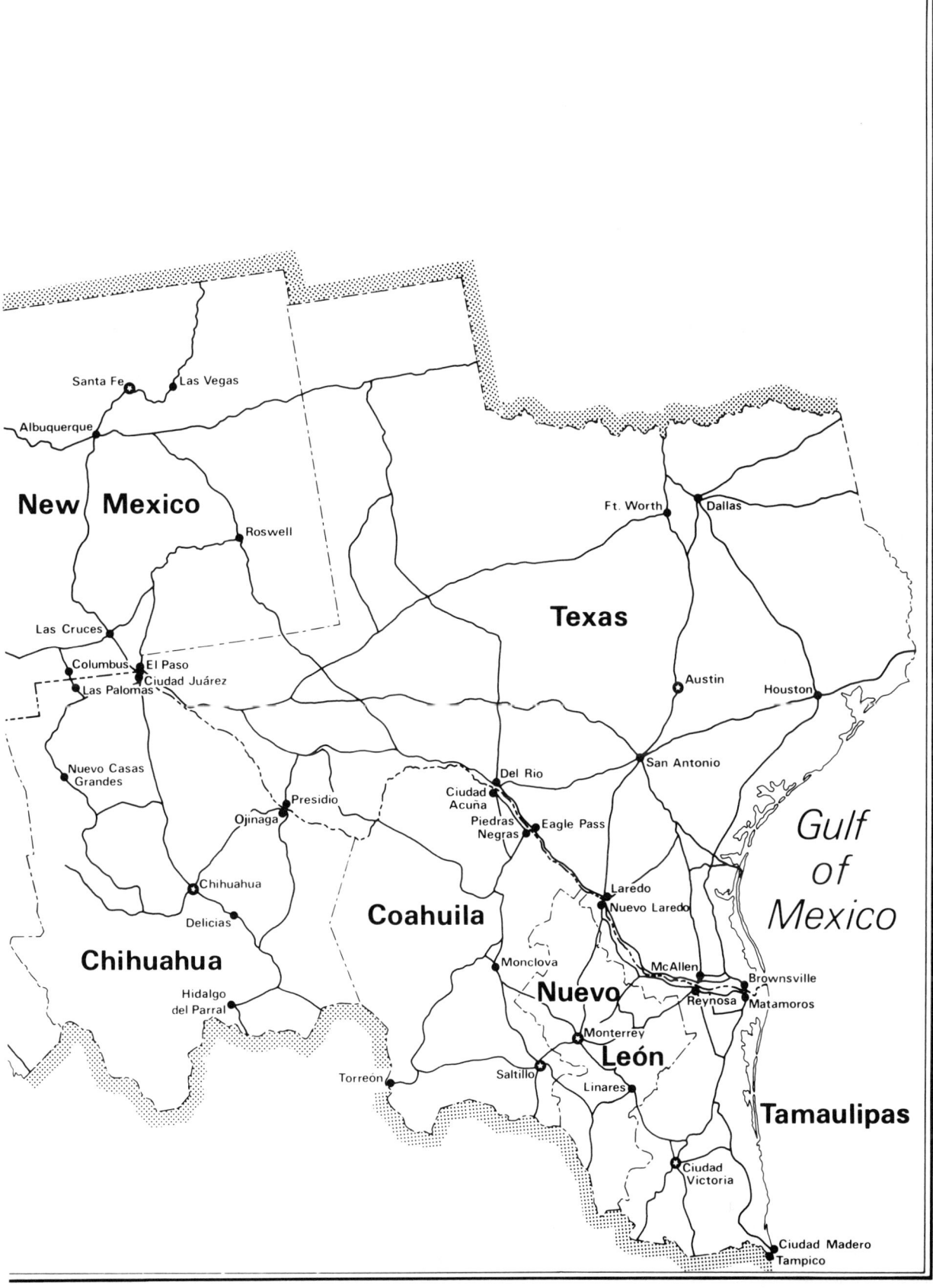

Preface

This volume constitutes a first effort to present binational quantitative time series for the Mexico–United States borderlands region. It is designed as a useful reference tool for individuals and institutions conducting business or scholarly investigation in the area. The abstract is part of UCLA's long-range borderlands program of research and publication. Other components of the borderlands project include a 14-volume United States-Mexico borderlands atlas, the publication of collections of interpretive essays on the region, and BorderLine, a computerized bibliography of the borderlands, headquartered at UCLA.

Consistent with the format of the *Statistical Abstract of Latin America*, also published by UCLA Latin American Center Publications, this work is divided into two major sections. The first part contains fifty-one statistical tables, organized into ten topical categories covering various aspects of the border region's economy and society. In thirty-two of the tables, data are aggregated for each state touching the international boundary, with the six Mexican states (Baja California Norte, Chihuahua, Coahuila, Nuevo León, Sonora, Tamaulipas), and the four U.S. states (Arizona, California, New Mexico, Texas) included. In these tables, states are coded A through J, so that each state is always represented by the same letter. Border State totals for each country and country totals are also included for comparative purposes. The second section, entitled "Development of Data," contains four short studies that apply quantitative techniques to border-related issues. Together, the tables and articles demonstrate the possibilities of creating a binational statistical database covering the borderlands.

Inherent in this project's design are assumptions concerning the definition of the borderlands as an area, and the extent to which binational data can be compared. Past delineations of a borderlands area have emphasized cultural, economic, or legal concepts.[1] For the purpose of the statistical presentation here, it was decided that a political categorization using state boundaries would be the most useful way to display the data. First, data on this level have been generated in both Mexico and the United States since the mid-nineteenth century, with many topics on which statistics are now collected having been defined in a consistent manner since 1900. Second, many of these topics are defined similarly among the various border states of each country, and between both countries as well. Third, below the national level, the most important formal governmental policies affecting the borderlands are composed and executed by states, rather than by other regionally defined entities.[2] Other political levels, such as national and local (municipio in Mexico, county and city in the United States), are represented in some of the tables, but these statistics lack either the regional focus, in the case of national data, or the binational comparability, in the case of local data, that the state-level aggregation provides. These national and local data are included because they constitute the only quantitative information available on many topics vitally affecting the borderlands, such as immigration, exchange rates, and some aspects of employment.

As to the question of comparing data internationally, the attempt has been made here to develop manageable binational categories. This task is not without difficulties, however, as a commentator on North American regionalism recently observed:

> Matching up most transnational numbers is beyond the scope of nations, much less a single author. No matter how much Montana looks and acts like Alberta, or New Mexico like Chihuahua—no matter how their problems, opportunities and people intertwine—the twain of their bureaucracies will only, with extreme difficulty, meet.[3]

---

[1] For a bibliographic overview of works emphasizing different definitional perspectives, see Ellwyn R. Stoddard, Richard L. Nostrand, and Jonathan P. West, eds., *Borderlands Sourcebook* (Norman: University of Oklahoma Press, 1983). A delimitation of the borderlands based on the cultural characteristics of its population is elaborated in Richard L. Nostrand, "The Hispanic-American Borderland: Delimitation of an American Culture Region," *Annals, Association of American Geographers* 60 (1970), 638–661. A classic view of the borderlands in economic terms is Ulises Irigoyen's *El problema económico de las fronteras mexicanas*, 2 vols. (México, D.F.: n.p., 1935), which focuses on the Mexican free-trade zone. More recent, and dealing largely with U.S. economic issues within the jurisdiction of the Southwest Regional Border Commission (counties touching the border and those adjacent to them), is Niles Hansen, *The Border Economy: Regional Development in the Southwest* (Austin: University of Texas Press, 1981). A legal perspective on the borderlands is offered by Robert W. Sutis's "The Extent of the Border," *Hastings Constitutional Law Quarterly* 1 (1974), 235–250, which examines the Immigration and Naturalization Service's authority to conduct warrantless searches within a "reasonable distance" from the international boundary.

[2] This statement is not intended to downplay the important *informal* relationships that local authorities on both sides of the border may have; these latter arrangements, however, are less susceptible to quantification.

[3] Joel Garreau, *The Nine Nations of North America* (New York: Avon, 1981), pp. xi–xii.

Indeed, many statistical categories are defined differently in Mexico and the United States, and many exist only on one side. Consequently, for the most part data have been presented that are comparable either in raw form or through simple metric conversion. For future volumes of this project, it is hoped that field research will facilitate the process of presenting binational data on topics such as education, health, and twin cities, which are largely excluded here because of lack of comparability.

A number of individuals assisted in the production of this volume. James W. Wilkie, UCLA Professor of History and Editor of the Statistical Abstract of Latin America Series; Ludwig Lauerhass, Jr., and Juan Gómez-Quiñones, Directors of the UCLA Latin American and Chicano Studies Research centers, respectively; and Paul Ganster, Coordinator of Mexico Programs at the Latin American Center, all provided encouragement for this project as part of UCLA's ongoing borderlands research program. During the data-gathering stage, Eudora Loh of the University Library's Public Affairs Service was particularly helpful in providing information about and access to quantitative sources. Juan Salcedo of the UCLA Graduate School of Management served as research assistant, compiling statistics and making calculations. Colleen Trujillo, Principal Editor and Production Manager at the UCLA Latin American Center, was extremely helpful both in making format suggestions and in guiding the work through production. Waldo W. Wilkie lent his experienced eye to the proofreading process. Finally, at the September 1983 Latin American Studies Association meeting in Mexico City, a paper summarizing the project was presented by Stephen Haber, to whom I am indebted for conveying the substantive suggestions of conference participants.

Peter L. Reich
Berkeley, California
September 1983

Part One
Statistical Time Series

1
Demography

Table 100

STATE POPULATION CENSUS SERIES, 10 SC, 1900-80

	State	1900	1910	1920	1930	1940	1950	1960	1970	1980
A.	BAJA CALIF. NORTE	7,583	9,760	23,537	48,327	78,907	226,965	520,165	870,421	1,225,436
B.	CHIHUAHUA	327,784	405,707	401,622	491,792	623,944	846,414	1,226,793	1,612,525	1,933,856
C.	COAHUILA	296,938	362,092	393,480	436,425	550,717	720,619	907,734	1,114,956	1,558,401
D.	NUEVO LEÓN	327,937	365,150	336,412	417,491	541,147	740,191	1,078,848	1,694,689	2,463,298
E.	SONORA	221,682	265,383	275,127	316,271	364,176	510,607	783,378	1,098,720	1,498,931
F.	TAMAULIPAS	218,948	249,641	286,904	344,039	458,832	718,167	1,024,182	1,456,858	1,924,934
	Mexico Border	1,400,872	1,657,733	1,717,082	2,054,345	2,617,723	3,762,963	5,541,100	7,848,169	10,604,856
	Mexico Total	13,607,272	15,160,369	14,334,780	16,552,722	19,653,552	25,791,013	34,923,129	48,225,230	67,382,581
G.	ARIZONA	122,931	204,354	334,162	435,573	499,261	749,587	1,302,161	1,770,900	2,718,215
H.	CALIFORNIA	1,485,053	2,377,549	3,426,861	5,677,251	6,907,387	10,586,223	15,717,204	19,953,134	23,667,902
I.	NEW MEXICO	195,310	327,301	360,350	423,317	531,818	681,187	951,023	1,016,000	1,302,894
J.	TEXAS	3,048,710	3,896,542	4,663,228	5,824,715	6,414,824	7,711,194	9,579,677	11,196,730	14,229,191
	U.S. Border	4,852,004	6,805,746	8,784,601	12,360,856	14,353,290	19,728,191	27,550,065	33,936,764	41,918,202
	U.S. Total	75,994,575	91,972,266	105,710,620	122,775,046	131,669,275	150,697,361	178,464,236	203,211,926	226,545,805

SOURCE: Mexico: II-IX *CGP*, 1900-80.
United States: *CP*, 1900-80.
1980 data from SPP, Mexico, Secretaría de Programacion y Presupuesto, *Programa núm.* 2 (March-June 1980).

Table 101

STATE PERCENTAGES OF BORDER AND NATIONAL POPULATION, 10 SC, 1900-80

	State	1900	1910	1920	1930	1940	1950	1960	1970	1980
A.	BAJA CALIF. NORTE									
	% Mexico Border	.5	.6	1.3	2.4	3.0	6.0	9.4	11.1	11.6
	% Mexico Total	.1	.1	.2	.3	.4	.9	1.5	1.8	1.8
B.	CHIHUAHUA									
	% Mexico Border	23.4	24.2	23.4	23.9	23.8	22.5	22.1	20.5	18.2
	% Mexico Total	2.4	2.7	2.8	3.0	3.2	3.3	3.5	3.3	2.8
C.	COAHUILA									
	% Mexico Border	21.2	21.6	22.9	21.2	21.0	19.2	16.4	14.2	14.7
	% Mexico Total	2.2	2.4	2.7	2.6	2.8	2.8	2.6	2.3	2.3
D.	NUEVO LEÓN									
	% Mexico Border	23.4	21.8	19.6	20.3	20.7	19.7	19.5	21.6	23.2
	% Mexico Total	2.4	2.4	2.3	2.5	2.8	2.9	3.1	3.5	3.7
E.	SONORA									
	% Mexico Border	15.8	15.8	16.0	15.3	13.9	13.6	14.1	14.0	14.1
	% Mexico Total	1.6	1.8	1.9	1.9	1.9	2.0	2.2	2.3	2.2
F.	TAMAULIPAS									
	% Mexico Border	15.6	14.9	16.7	16.7	17.2	19.1	18.5	13.0	18.1
	% Mexico Total	1.6	1.6	2.0	2.1	2.3	2.8	2.9	3.0	2.9
	Mexico Border									
	% Mexico Total	10.3	10.9	12.0	12.4	13.3	14.6	15.9	16.3	15.7
G.	ARIZONA									
	% U.S. Border	2.5	3.0	3.8	3.5	3.5	3.8	4.7	5.2	6.5
	% U.S. Total	.2	.2	.3	.4	.4	.5	.7	.9	1.2
H.	CALIFORNIA									
	% U.S. Border	30.6	35.0	39.0	45.9	48.1	53.7	57.0	58.8	56.5
	% U.S. Total	2.0	2.6	3.2	4.6	5.2	7.0	8.8	9.8	10.4
I.	NEW MEXICO									
	% U.S. Border	4.0	4.8	4.1	3.4	3.7	3.5	3.5	3.0	3.1
	% U.S. Total	.3	.4	.3	.3	.4	.4	.5	.5	.6
J.	TEXAS									
	% U.S. Border	62.8	57.3	53.1	47.1	44.7	39.1	34.8	33.0	33.9
	% U.S. Total	4.0	4.2	4.4	4.7	4.9	5.1	5.4	5.5	6.3
	U.S. Border									
	% U.S. Total	6.4	7.4	8.3	10.1	10.9	13.1	15.4	16.7	18.5

SOURCE: Calculated from table 100 above.

Table 102

POPULATION DENSITY, 10 SC, 1900-80

PART I. Per km^2

	State	1900	1910	1920	1930	1940	1950	1960	1970	1980
A.	BAJA CALIF. NORTE	.1	.1	.3	.7	1.1	3.2	7.4	12.4	17.5
B.	CHIHUAHUA	1.4	1.7	1.6	2.0	2.5	3.5	5.0	6.5	7.8
C.	COAHUILA	1.8	2.2	2.6	2.9	3.7	4.8	6.0	7.4	10.3
D.	NUEVO LEÓN	5.3	5.6	5.2	6.4	8.3	11.4	16.7	26.3	38.1
E.	SONORA	1.1	1.3	1.5	1.7	2.0	2.8	4.2	5.9	8.1
F.	TAMAULIPAS	2.6	3.1	3.6	4.3	5.8	9.0	12.8	18.3	24.1
	MEXICO BORDER	1.8	2.1	2.2	2.6	3.3	3.9	7.0	9.9	13.3
	Mexico Total	6.8	7.6	7.3	8.4	10.0	13.1	17.8	24.5	33.7
G.	ARIZONA	.4	.7	1.1	1.5	1.7	2.5	4.4	6.0	9.3
H.	CALIFORNIA	3.7	5.9	8.5	14.0	17.0	26.1	38.8	49.3	58.5
I.	NEW MEXICO	.6	1.0	1.1	1.4	1.7	2.2	3.0	3.2	4.1
J.	TEXAS	4.5	5.7	6.9	8.5	9.4	11.3	14.0	16.5	21.0
	U.S. Border	2.9	4.0	5.2	7.3	8.5	11.6	16.2	20.0	24.8
	U.S. Total	9.9	12.0	13.7	15.9	17.1	19.6	19.5	22.2	24.7

PART II. Per Square Mile

	State	1900	1910	1920	1930	1940	1950	1960	1970	1980
A.	BAJA CALIF. NORTE	.3	.3	.8	1.8	2.8	8.3	19.2	32.1	45.3
B.	CHIHUAHUA	3.6	4.4	4.1	5.2	6.5	9.1	12.9	16.8	20.2
C.	COAHUILA	4.7	5.7	6.7	7.5	9.6	12.4	15.5	19.2	26.7
D.	NUEVO LEON	13.7	14.5	13.5	16.6	21.5	29.5	43.2	68.1	98.7
E.	SONORA	2.8	3.4	3.9	4.4	5.2	7.3	10.9	15.3	21.0
F.	TAMAULIPAS	6.7	8.0	9.3	11.1	15.0	23.3	33.2	47.4	62.4
	Mexico Border	4.7	5.4	5.7	6.7	8.5	10.1	18.1	25.6	34.4
	Mexico Total	17.6	19.7	18.9	21.8	25.9	33.9	46.1	63.5	87.3
G.	ARIZONA	1.1	1.8	2.9	3.8	4.4	6.6	11.5	15.6	24.0
H.	CALIFORNIA	9.5	15.3	22.0	36.2	44.1	67.5	100.4	126.6	151.4
I.	NEW MEXICO	1.6	2.7	2.9	3.5	4.4	5.6	7.8	8.4	10.7
J.	TEXAS	11.6	14.8	17.8	22.1	24.3	29.3	36.4	42.7	54.3
	U.S. Border	7.4	10.4	13.4	18.9	21.9	30.1	42.1	51.9	64.2
	U.S. Total	25.6	31.0	35.6	41.2	44.2	50.7	50.6[a]	57.5	64.1

a. First year for which data include Alaska and Hawaii.

SOURCE: Mexico: *CGP*, 1900-80.
          United States: *HSUS*, 1975, vol. I, series A, pp. 195-209.

Table 103

STATE POPULATION PROJECTIONS, 10 SC, 1970-2000

(T)

	State	1970	1980	1990	2000
A.	BAJA CALIF. NORTE	870	1,227	2,000	3.256
B.	CHIHUAHUA	1,613	1,935	2,336	2,819
C.	COAHUILA	1,115	1,561	2,030	2,275
D.	NUEVO LEÓN	1,695	2.464	3,476	4,537
E.	SONORA	1,099	1,498	2,003	2,552
F.	TAMAULIPAS	1,457	1,925	2,448	3,065
	Mexico Border	7,849	10,610	14,333	18,504
	Mexico Total	48,225	67,406	88,400	102,000
G.	ARIZONA	1,775	2,715	3,449	4,041
H.	CALIFORNIA	19,971	23,533	26,710	29,300
I.	NEW MEXICO	1,011	1,295	1,520	1,697
J.	TEXAS	11,199	14,170	16,479	18,441
	U.S. Border	33,956	41,713	48,158	53,479
	U.S. Total	203,306	226,505	248,249	265,378

SOURCE: Security Pacific National Bank, *U.S.-Mexican Border Region Economic Report*, December, 1981.

Table 104

TWIN CITY[1] POPULATIONS, 1900-70

(N)

City, State	1900	1910	1920	1930	1940	1950	1960	1970
Matamoros, Tamps.	8,347	7,390	9,215	9,733	15,699	45,737	143,043	186,146
Brownsville, Tex.	6,305	10,517	11,791	22,021	22,083	36,066	48,040	52,522
Reynosa, Tamps.	1,915	1,475	2,107	4,840	9,412	34,076	134,869	150,786
McAllen, Tex.	~	~	5,331	9,074	11.877	20,067	32,728	37,636
Nuevo Laredo, Tamps.	6,548	8,143	14,998	21,636	28,872	57,669	96,043	151,253
Laredo, Tex.	13,429	14,855	22,710	32,618	39,274	51,510	60,678	69,024
Piedras Negras, Coah.	7,888	8,518	6,941	15,878	15,663	27,578	48,408	46,698
Eagle Pass, Tex.	~	3,536	5,765	5,059	6,459	7,267	12,094	15,364
Ciudad Juárez, Chih.	8,218	10,621	19,457	39,669	48,881	122,566	276,995	424,135
El Paso, Tex.	15,906	39,279	77,560	102,421	96,810	130,485	276,687	322,261
Nogales, Son.	2,738	3.117	13,445	14,061	13,866	24,480	39,812	53,494
Nogales, Ariz.	~	3,514	5,199	6,006	5,135	6,153	7,286	8,946
Mexicali, B.C.	~	462	6,782	14,842	18,775	64,658	281,333	396,324
Calexico, Calif.	~	797	6,223	6,299	5,415	6,433	7,992	10,625
Tijuana, B.C.	242	733	1,028	8,384	16,486	59,950	165,690	340,583
San Diego, Calif.	17,700	39,978	74,683	147,897	203,341	334,387	573,224	697,027

1. Contiguous or near-contiguous cities separated by the Mexican-U.S. border. First city listed is Mexican; second is U.S.

SOURCE: Mexico: *CGP*, 1900-70.
United States: *CP*, 1900-70; San Diego Federal Writers' Project, *San Diego, a California City* (San Diego: San Diego Historical Society, 1937), p. 49.

Table 105

MEXICO BORDER CITY POPULATION, BY STATE OF ORIGIN, 32 SC, 1970

State	Border City Total	Juárez	Mexicali	Tijuana	Ensenada	Matamoros	Nuevo Laredo	Reynosa
Aguascalientes	9,258	3,856	1,283	2,232	349	442	581	515
Baja California	1,031	628	~	~	~	145	174	84
Baja California Territory	9,476	60	2,757	1,794	4,736	41	34	54
Campeche	606	67	63	128	76	84	112	76
Coahuila	41,512	17,801	2,029	2,627	441	4,199	9,711	4,704
Colima	5,727	190	922	2,690	1,606	101	112	106
Chiapas	1,241	169	142	352	123	89	219	147
Chihuahua	11,439	~	2,749	5,358	1,295	557	890	590
Distrito Federal	24,998	3,125	3,917	10,699	2,401	1,646	1,924	1,286
Durango	51,769	31,885	6,117	7,095	1,455	1,301	2,267	1,649
Guanajuato	36,964	4,782	11,260	8,560	1,483	3,690	3,421	3,768
Guerrero	2,905	328	403	1,068	490	182	297	137
Hidalgo	2,088	193	276	542	185	324	269	299
Jalisco	89,325	5,315	25,212	44,307	7,620	2,401	2,277	2,193
México	10,608	1,757	1,693	4,289	741	565	860	703
Michoacán	40,850	1,071	15,058	16,128	3,814	1,452	1,801	1,526
Morelos	4,219	739	964	1,447	320	235	243	271
Nayarit	15,885	174	6,097	7,888	1,389	107	109	121
Nuevo León	42,937	1,135	620	965	233	9,247	14,610	16,127
Oaxaca	2,677	349	564	664	517	214	184	185
Puebla	3,014	331	492	1,052	285	279	234	341
Querétaro	1,589	129	226	362	105	408	150	209
Quintana Roo	421	49	125	104	66	24	35	18
San Luis Potosí	22,985	1,070	732	1,330	264	7,742	6,305	5,542
Sinaloa	41,489	615	20,414	15,815	4,148	170	177	150
Sonora	36,762	764	20,216	11,288	4,040	167	172	115
Tabasco	684	50	104	130	43	130	95	132
Tamaulipas	4,158	1,243	1,193	1,419	303	~	~	~
Tlaxcala	721	54	173	208	55	101	69	61
Veracruz	8,496	591	694	1,253	506	1,274	821	3,357
Yucatán	1,300	164	220	441	96	89	219	71
Zacatecas	44,705	18,449	8,859	9,526	2,036	1,833	1,892	2,110
Mexico Total	571,839	97,133	135,574	161,761	41,221	39,239	50,264	46,647

SOURCE: *LFN*, table III-2.

Table 106

PERSONS OF MEXICAN ORIGIN OR DESCENT IN THE UNITED STATES,[1]
4 SC, 1970 AND 1980

		1970			1980		
		Persons of Mexican Origin (N)	As % of Hispanics[2]	As % of General Population	Persons of Mexican Origin (N)	As % of Hispanics[2]	As % of General Population
G.	ARIZONA	240,025	90.6	13.6	396,410	89.9	14.6
H.	CALIFORNIA	1,856,841	78.4	9.3	3,637,466	80.0	15.4
I.	NEW MEXICO	119,049	38.6	11.7	233,772	49.9	17.9
J.	TEXAS	1,619,252	88.0	14.5	2,752,487	92.2	19.3
	U.S. Border	3,835,166	80.2	11.3	7,020,435	83.1	16.7
	U.S. Total	4,532,552	50.0	2.2	8,740,439	59.8	3.9

1. Persons who self-identified on census questionnaire as being of Mexican origin or descent. 1970 data may not be directly comparable with 1980 data because of better coverage of surveyed population in latter year.
2. Persons who self-identified on census questionnaire as being of "Spanish" origin or descent.

SOURCE: *CP*, 1970 Supplementary Report, "Persons of Spanish Ancestry"; and
CP, 1980 Supplementary Report, "Persons of Spanish Origin by State."

2
Vital Statistics

Table 200
BIRTHS, BY STATE, 1930-81
(N)

	State	1930	1931	1932	1933	1934	1935	1936	1937	1938	1939
A.	BAJA CALIF. NORTE	3,375	2,005	2,070	1,940	2,121	2,104	3,899	2,635	2,791	3,198
B.	CHIHUAHUA	20,906	21,436	21,404	21,458	23,874	22,628	23,929	26,126	24,342	24,459
C.	COAHUILA	19,817	20,374	20,159	21,784	27,380	24,247	26,260	27,328	26,393	32,296
D.	NUEVO LEÓN	16,298	19,750	19,472	18,699	22,753	20,472	24,509	26,038	23,411	24,738
E.	SONORA	12,006	12,228	13,546	14,014	12,272	10,643	11,166	22,483	16,241	17,136
F.	TAMAULIPAS	15,202	12,862	12,566	12,505	17,874	13,876	17,096	17,702	15,789	17,139
	Mexico Border	87,604	88,655	89,217	90,400	106,274	93,961	106,859	122,312	108,967	118,966
	Mexico Total	819,814	738,399	743,150	737,020	787,314	764,326	791,725	826,307	765,547	801,531
G.	ARIZONA	10,376	9,369	8,523	8,125	8,492	9,139	9,545	10,494	10,878	10,928
H.	CALIFORNIA	84,206	81,426	78,093	75,036	78,346	80,131	84,502	94,230	101,844	103,453
I.	NEW MEXICO	12,115	12,322	12,391	12,304	12,769	13,190	12,907	13,837	14,290	14,215
J.	TEXAS	~a	~a	~a	107,950	116,603	114,721	111,602	116,057	121,156	121,049
	U.S. Border	106,697	103,117	99,007	203,415	216,210	217,180	218,556	234,618	248,168	249,645
	U.S. Total	2,203,958	2,112,760	2,074,042	2,081,232	2,167,636	2,155,105	2,144,790	2,203,337	2,286,962	2,265,588

Table 200 (Continued)
BIRTHS, BY STATE, 1930-81
(N)

	State	1940	1941	1942	1943	1944	1945	1946	1947	1948	1949
A.	BAJA CALIF. NORTE	3,385	3,771	4,269	4,868	5,077	5,853	6,328	7,961	8,579	9,011
B.	CHIHUAHUA	30,767	27,839	29,602	29,241	29,678	29,726	29,639	32,422	34,002	34,014
C.	COAHUILA	35,003	28,454	35,150	34,131	33,470	35,963	34,043	33,398	35,376	36,049
D.	NUEVO LEÓN	24,523	26,371	26,646	27,346	27,595	29,105	30,440	29,101	30,789	32,348
E.	SONORA	18,629	17,891	19,578	22,371	20,401	20,993	20,507	22,602	22,731	23,358
F.	TAMAULIPAS	16,722	17,827	29,545	20,848	23,133	23,307	25,611	25,043	27,527	30,795
	Mexico Border	129,029	122,153	144,790	138,805	139,354	144,947	146,568	150,527	159,004	165,575
	Mexico Total	875,471	878,935	940,067	963,317	958,119	999,093	994,838	1,079,816	1,090,867	1,123,358
G.	ARIZONA	11,503	11,425	12,664	14,297	14,225	13,348	16,345	19,153	19,195	17,520
H.	CALIFORNIA	112,287	125,190	154,567	174,420	179,123	184,380	218,484	245,889	240,702	224,785
I.	NEW MEXICO	14,792	14,738	14,129	15,211	15,585	15,306	18,087	20,322	20,519	20,118
J.	TEXAS	127,072	136,782	144,742	164,513	165,900	157,915	181,579	198,662	197,750	175,709
	U.S. Border	265,654	288,135	326,102	368,441	374,833	370,949	434,495	484,026	478,166	438,132
	U.S. Total	2,360,399	2,513,427	2,808,996	2,934,860	2,794,800	2,735,456	3,288,672	3,699,940	3,535,068	3,083,721

Ch. 2, Vital Statistics   13

Table 200 (Continued)

BIRTHS, BY STATE, 10 SC, 1930-81
(N)

	State	1950	1951	1952	1953	1954	1955	1956	1957	1958	1959
A.	BAJA CALIF. NORTE	11,017	12,034	13,492	16,336	17,672	19,733	20,744	22,608	23,990	24,631
B.	CHIHUAHUA	36,112	38,350	37,834	40,318	43,622	44,310	45,999	50,576	49,655	53,151
C.	COAHUILA	35,641	36,484	35,211	36,292	37,812	40,651	39,770	41,130	40,227	44,478
D.	NUEVO LEÓN	32,416	33,207	33,945	32,857	37,280	38,978	40,649	43,839	43,993	48,575
E.	SONORA	25,772	25,556	26,210	30,141	32,369	32,850	35,089	36,853	37,668	38,268
F.	TAMAULIPAS	30,832	32,567	33,668	33,488	41,996	41,923	42,475	43,047	42,053	43,820
	Mexico Border	171,790	178,198	180,360	189,432	210,751	218,445	224,726	238,063	237,586	252,923
	Mexico Total	1,174,947	1,183,788	1,195,209	1,261,775	1,339,837	1,377,917	1,427,722	1,485,202	1,447,578	1,589,606
G.	ARIZONA	23,013	22,536	26,960	28,011	29,071	29,700	30,036	34,015	35,240	34,975
H.	CALIFORNIA	247,146	260,758	283,929	299,962	308,706	315,901	333,144	353,549	352,195	355,288
I.	NEW MEXICO	23,468	23,664	25,535	26,424	26,972	27,022	26,406	29,182	29,876	29,509
J.	TEXAS	212,531	217,782	234,526	243,775	246,661	246,727	246,372	257,232	252,477	252,193
	U.S. Border	506,158	524,740	570,950	598,172	611,410	619,350	636,318	673,981	669,788	671,965
	U.S. Total	3,631,512	3,750,850[b]	3,913,115	3,964,750	4,078,055	4,104,112	4,163,090	4,308,351	4,255,005[b]	4,244,796

Table 200 (Continued)

BIRTHS, BY STATE, 10 SC, 1930-81
(N)

	State	1960	1961	1962	1963	1964	1965	1966	1967	1968	1969
A.	BAJA CALIF. NORTE	25,241	13,085	29,049	31,508	32,059	32,660	34,025	33,452	36,077	37,442
B.	CHIHUAHUA	55,347	57,821	60,019	61,443	62,203	64,902	63,809	65,423	66,708	67,224
C.	COAHUILA	44,813	45,517	45,262	45,599	48,279	52,197	52,933	53,890	54,947	56,752
D.	NUEVO LEÓN	51,012	54,287	54,760	55,576	61,334	61,795	65,255	66,947	89,680	72,029
E.	SONORA	40,210	40,702	41,440	42,851	43,490	44,864	47,692	46,886	48,857	50,357
F.	TAMAULIPAS	43,648	45,812	45,550	49,246	53,173	51,964	54,897	52,221	58,284	56,279
	Mexico Border	260,271	257,224	276,080	286,223	300,586	308,382	318,611	318,819	354,553	340,083
	Mexico Total	1,608,174	1,647,006	1,705,481	1,756,624	1,849,408	1,888,171	1,954,340	1,981,363	2,058,251	2,088,902
G.	ARIZONA	36,760	36,906	37,864	36,785	36,304	33,770	32,556	32,089	32,716	34,100
H.	CALIFORNIA	372,210	381,606	378,880	371,813	374,972	352,146	338,184	340,661	339,760	352,966
I.	NEW MEXICO	30,680	30,680	29,222	27,228	26,838	24,480	22,324	21,386	20,346	21,326
J.	TEXAS	249,142	246,444	246,500	233,931	234,100	217,659	208,144	206,104	211,272	226,942
	U.S. Border	688,792	695,636	692,466	669,757	672,214	628,055	601,208	600,240	604,094	635,334
	U.S. Total	4,257,850	4,268,326	4,167,362	4,081,000	4,027,490	3,760,358	3,606,274	3,520,959	3,501,564	3,600,206

Table 200 (Continued)
BIRTHS, BY STATE, 10 SC, 1930-81
(N)

	State	1970	1971	1972	1973	1974	1975	1976	1977	1978	1979	1980	1981
A.	BAJA CALIF. NORTE	38,206	39,820	42,705	47,519	43,079	40,995	38,921	37,390	34,920	38,820	?	?
B.	CHIHUAHUA	66,238	68,821	69,523	71,378	76,760	70,946	68,399	65,798	61,294	63,482	?	?
C.	COAHUILA	57,073	61,720	58,717	67,117	62,708	60,838	58,314	57,206	53,741	60,863	?	?
D.	NUEVO LEÓN	74,408	79,780	82,365	85,727	92,499	86,886	81,938	73,589	82,246	77,922	?	?
E.	SONORA	50,926	51,703	52,506	55,906	55,491	53,793	53,124	50,641	48,240	50,945	?	?
F.	TAMAULIPAS	57,997	58,695	72,921	76,408	69,951	61,078	58,319	61,523	59,889	66,409	?	?
	Mexico Border	344,848	360,539	378,737	404,055	400,488	374,536	359,015	346,147	340,930	358,441	?	?
	Mexico Total	2,121,197	2,218,821	2,346,002	2,572,287	2,607,450	2,427,058	2,370,025	2,402,418	2,346,862	2,448,774		
G.	ARIZONA	37,672	38,398	37,493	37,852	39,841	39,578	40,044	41,822	43,014	46,709	50,173	51,322
H.	CALIFORNIA	362,756	329,954	306,470	298,086	311,820	317,423	332,238	347,436	356,196	379,422	401,581	422,066
I.	NEW MEXICO	22,098	22,200	20,749	20,578	21,319	21,036	21,666	22,600	23,266	25,558	25,661	28,262
J.	TEXAS	231,036	229,152	214,605	218,742	211,063	215,665	227,409	234,985	242,548	254,508	268,717	287,272
	U.S. Border	653,562	619,704	579,317	575,258	584,043	593,702	621,357	646,843	665,024	706,197	746,132	788,922
	U.S. Total	3,731,386[b]	3,555,970[b]	3,258,411	3,146,125	3,159,958	3,144,198	3,167,788	3,326,632	3,333,279	3,494,398	3,598,000[‡]	3,646,000[‡]

a. Not in registration area.
b. Based on 50% sample.

SOURCE: Mexico: *AEM*, 1938-81, various tables.
United States: *SAUS*, 1930-80; *VSSR*, 1934-37; *VSUS*, 1937-78; *MVSR*, Vol. 30,
No. 13 (Dec. 20, 1982), and Vol. 30, No. 6 (Sept. 29, 1981) various tables.

Table 201

BIRTH RATE, BY STATE, 10 SC, 1930-81

(PTI)

	State	1930	1931	1932	1933	1934	1935	1936	1937	1938	1939
A.	BAJA CALIF. NORTE	69.1	40.6	40.9	37.6	40.3	39.2	71.3	47.4	49.4	42.8
B.	CHIHUAHUA	42.3	42.3	41.3	40.6	44.3	41.1	42.7	45.9	42.1	44.8
C.	COAHUILA	42.3	45.3	43.7	46.3	57.1	49.6	52.8	54.0	51.3	60.0
D.	NUEVO LEÓN	38.9	46.0	44.2	41.7	49.7	43.8	51.6	53.9	47.7	46.7
E.	SONORA	37.9	37.6	40.6	41.2	35.4	30.1	31.0	61.5	43.7	49.9
F.	TAMAULIPAS	44.1	36.3	34.6	33.7	47.3	36.0	43.6	44.4	39.0	38.6
	Mexico Border	42.8	~	~	~	~	~	~	~	~	~
	Mexico Total	49.4	43.3	42.5	41.4	43.4	41.3	42.0	43.1	39.3	44.6
G.	ARIZONA	24.0	22.0	20.3	19.7	20.9	22.5	23.5	25.5	26.4	26.0
H.	CALIFORNIA	14.8	14.1	13.4	12.8	13.2	13.4	13.9	15.3	16.5	16.8
I.	NEW MEXICO	28.6	29.1	29.4	29.2	30.3	31.3	30.6	32.8	33.9	33.7
J.	TEXAS	~	~	~	18.0	19.3	18.9	18.2	18.8	19.6	19.6
	U.S. Border	8.6	~	~	~	~	~	~	~	~	~
	U.S. Total	18.9	18.0	17.4	16.5	17.1	16.9	16.7	17.0	17.6	17.4

Table 201 (Continued)

BIRTH RATE, BY STATE, 10 SC, 1930-81

(PTI)

	State	1940	1941	1942	1943	1944	1945	1946	1947	1948	1949
A.	BAJA CALIF. NORTE	42.2	44.7	48.4	52.5	52.5	57.6	59.7	71.3	72.5	71.6
B.	CHIHUAHUA	48.9	43.0	44.5	42.8	42.3	41.2	40.2	42.7	43.5	42.1
C.	COAHUILA	63.1	49.6	59.4	55.7	52.7	54.4	49.9	47.4	48.5	47.8
D.	NUEVO LEÓN	44.9	46.7	45.6	45.1	44.0	44.6	44.8	41.1	41.8	42.3
E.	SONORA	50.9	47.3	50.2	55.1	48.7	48.3	45.7	48.4	46.8	46.3
F.	TAMAULIPAS	36.1	37.7	60.8	41.1	44.4	43.2	46.0	43.5	46.2	49.8
	Mexico Border	49.3	~	~	~	~	~	~	~	~	~
	Mexico Total	44.3	43.5	45.5	45.5	44.2	44.9	43.7	46.1	45.2	45.2
G.	ARIZONA	22.8	22.7	24.7	25.5	24.8	25.2	27.7	29.7	27.3	27.9
H.	CALIFORNIA	16.2	17.7	21.3	23.0	22.5	22.0	23.6	25.1	23.2	23.4
I.	NEW MEXICO	27.6	27.6	27.3	31.1	32.1	32.6	35.1	37.2	35.9	34.2
J.	TEXAS	19.8	21.3	22.5	26.3	26.5	25.2	26.6	28.0	26.8	26.4
	U.S. Border	18.5	~	~	~	~	~	~	~	~	~
	U.S. Total	17.9	18.9	20.9	21.5	20.2	19.6	23.3	25.8	24.2	24.0

Table 201 (Continued)

BIRTH RATE, BY STATE, 10 SC, 1930-81

(PTI)

	State	1950	1951	1952	1953	1954	1955	1956	1957	1958	1959
A.	BAJA CALIF. NORTE	48.2	47.5	48.1	52.5	51.2	51.6	48.9	49.5	46.0	42.6
B.	CHIHUAHUA	42.6	43.9	42.0	43.5	45.7	45.0	45.4	47.9	46.2	48.0
C.	COAHUILA	49.4	49.2	46.3	46.5	47.2	49.4	47.1	47.3	45.2	48.7
D.	NUEVO LEÓN	43.7	43.4	43.1	40.4	44.5	45.1	45.6	48.0	46.5	49.8
E.	SONORA	50.4	48.3	48.0	53.4	55.4	54.4	56.3	57.3	56.6	55.6
F.	TAMAULIPAS	42.8	43.3	42.8	40.8	49.0	46.8	45.4	44.2	41.2	41.1
	Mexico Border	45.7	~	~	~	~	~	~	~	~	~
	Mexico Total	45.6	44.6	43.8	45.0	46.4	46.4	46.8	46.9	44.8	47.7
G.	ARIZONA	30.7	30.5	31.0[a]	31.3[a]	31.3[a]	28.8	29.1	31.6	30.0	29.7
H.	CALIFORNIA	23.3	23.8	24.1[a]	24.8[a]	24.7[a]	24.4	25.0	25.5	24.7	24.7
I.	NEW MEXICO	34.5	35.4	34.7[a]	34.5[a]	34.7[a]	34.1	34.7	35.9	34.9	35.8
J.	TEXAS	27.6	28.0	28.7[a]	29.0[a]	29.1[a]	28.1	28.3	28.0	27.1	26.8
	U.S. Border	25.7	~	~	~	~	~	~	~	~	~
	U.S. Total	24.1	24.9	25.1[a]	25.0[a]	25.3[a]	25.0	25.2	25.3	24.6	24.1

Table 201 (Continued)

BIRTH RATE, BY STATE, 10 SC, 1930-81

(PTI)

	State	1960	1961	1962	1963	1964	1965	1966	1967	1968	1969
A.	BAJA CALIF. NORTE	48.3	46.0	47.1	47.3	44.7	42.1	40.9	37.3	37.3	35.9
B.	CHIHUAHUA	45.0	45.3	45.3	43.5	42.2	42.2	39.7	39.0	38.1	36.8
C.	COAHUILA	49.3	47.5	47.5	43.5	42.2	47.4	46.8	46.4	46.1	46.3
D.	NUEVO LEÓN	47.2	48.3	47.0	43.4	45.8	44.1	44.5	43.6	55.9	42.9
E.	SONORA	51.2	49.7	48.4	45.4	44.0	43.3	44.0	41.3	41.0	40.3
F.	TAMAULIPAS	42.5	43.1	41.3	41.5	43.2	40.6	41.3	37.9	40.7	37.8
	Mexico Border	47.0	~	~	~	~	~	~	~	~	~
	Mexico Total	46.0	45.6	45.8	44.1	44.8	44.2	44.3	43.4	43.5	42.7
G.	ARIZONA	28.2	26.3	25.8	24.5	23.4	21.1	20.1	19.8	19.7	20.2
H.	CALIFORNIA	23.7	23.2	22.3	21.7	20.7	19.1	17.9	17.6	17.6	18.2
I.	NEW MEXICO	32.3	31.2	29.9	28.1	26.5	23.6	21.8	21.3	20.2	21.6
J.	TEXAS	26.0	25.0	24.3	23.3	22.5	20.4	19.4	19.1	19.3	20.3
	U.S. Border	25.0	~	~	~	~	~	~	~	~	~
	U.S. Total	23.7	23.3	22.4	21.7	21.0	19.4	18.4	17.8	17.5	17.8

Ch. 2, Vital Statistics

Table 201 (Continued)

BIRTH RATE, BY STATE, 10 SC, 1930-81

(PTI)

	State	1970	1971	1972	1973	1974	1975	1976	1977	1978	1979	1980	1981
A.	BAJA CALIF. NORTE	43.1	41.3	41.8	44.2	38.1	35.5	29.0	31.1	34.3	31.7	~	~
B.	CHIHUAHUA	40.9	39.7	38.8	38.8	40.6	36.0	24.4	29.0	31.6	30.9	~	~
C.	COAHUILA	50.1	52.1	48.2	53.9	49.2	44.8	29.0	25.7	28.2	25.6	~	~
D.	NUEVO LEÓN	43.4	42.9	42.1	41.9	43.2	39.3	27.2	31.4	29.0	31.6	~	~
E.	SONORA	46.0	43.6	42.5	43.7	42.0	38.8	26.1	28.2	30.4	29.5	~	~
F.	TAMAULIPAS	39.4	37.3	44.4	44.9	39.6	33.7	30.9	30.1	31.6	29.2	~	~
	Mexico Border	43.9	~	~	~	~	~	27.4	29.2	30.5	29.7	~	
	Mexico Total	43.4	42.5	43.2	45.8	44.9	40.4	26.0	26.4	27.9	27.5		
G.	ARIZONA	21.3	20.6	19.1	18.4	18.5	17.8	17.6	18.2	18.2	19.1	18.4	18.4
H.	CALIFORNIA	18.2	16.3	15.0	14.5	14.9	15.0	15.4	15.9	16.0	16.7	16.9	17.4
I.	NEW MEXICO	21.8	21.2	19.3	18.8	19.0	18.3	18.9	19.4	19.7	20.6	19.7	21.3
J.	TEXAS	20.6	20.1	18.5	17.8	17.5	17.6	17.5	17.9	18.2	19.0	18.8	19.5
	U.S. Border	19.3	~	~	~	~	~	~	~	~	~	17.8	~
	U.S. Total	18.4	17.2	15.6	14.9	14.9	14.8	14.8	15.4	15.3	15.9	15.8	15.9

a. Based on 50% sample.

SOURCE: Mexico: *AEM*, 1938-81, various tables.
United States: *SAUS*, 1930-81; *VSSR*, 1934-37; *VSUS*, 1937-78; *MVSR*, Vol. 30,
No. 13 (Dec. 20, 1982), and Vol. 30, No. 2 (May 29, 1981), various tables.

Table 202

BIRTHS IN THE UNITED STATES BY MEXICAN ORIGIN OF PARENTS,[1] 2 SC, 1979

	State	Mexican Origin of Father			Mexican Origin of Mother		
		N	As % of Hispanic Origin[2]	As % of All Births	N	As % of Hispanic Origin[3]	As % of All Births
G.	ARIZONA[4]	10,060	91.2	21.5	10,007	90.8	21.4
H.	CALIFORNIA[4]	88,841	89.6	23.4	87,195	89.1	23.0
	U.S. Total	119,756	63.5	7.4	117,989	60.1	7.3

1. Persons who self-identified on census questionnaire as being of Mexican origin or descent.
2. Births from fathers who self-identified on census questionnaire as being of Spanish origin or descent.
3. Births from mothers who self-identified on census questionnaire as being of Spanish origin or descent.
4. Only states reporting.

SOURCE: Stephanie J. Ventura, "Births of Hispanic Parentage, 1979," in *MVSR*, Vol. 31, No. 2, Supplement, May 13, 1982.

Table 203
DEATHS, BY STATE, 10 SC, 1930-81
(N)

	State	1930	1931	1932	1933	1934	1935	1936	1937	1938	1939
A.	BAJA CALIF. NORTE	1,103	956	880	892	1,082	915	1,271	1,349	1,040	1,249
B.	CHIHUAHUA	9,681	9,877	10,605	10,465	12,039	11,909	10,635	12,823	11,424	11,192
C.	COAHUILA	11,021	12,778	11,713	11,856	11,786	10,780	10,968	13,992	11,756	12,485
D.	NUEVO LEÓN	8,448	9,506	10,783	10,393	10,648	9,894	8,712	10,517	9,486	9,565
E.	SONORA	5,776	5,608	5,920	5,925	6,463	6,484	6,476	7,392	6,410	7,699
F.	TAMAULIPAS	5,662	6,175	6,973	8,324	6,875	6,158	6,231	6,669	6,488	5,986
	Mexico Border	41,691	44,910	46,874	47,855	48,893	46,140	44,293	52,742	46,604	48,176
	Mexico Total	441,717	437,038	447,532	449,149	422,595	408,471	432,673	456,540	436,963	444,032
G.	ARIZONA	6,679	6,074	5,420	5,539	5,647	6,077	6,551	6,919	6,002	5,851
H.	CALIFORNIA	66,249	67,410	67,680	68,036	68,095	72,456	72,656	80,256	76,187	77,130
I.	NEW MEXICO	6,596	6,156	5,968	5,824	6,115	6,272	6,248	6,422	5,962	5,917
J.	TEXAS	~a	~a	~a	58,948	59,731	61,663	65,803	65,448	60,208	60,218
	U.S. Border	79,524	79,640	79,068	138,347	139,588	146,468	151,258	159,045	148,359	149,116
	U.S. Total	1,343,356	1,322,587	1,308,529	1,342,106	1,396,903	1,392,752	1,479,228	1,450,427	1,381,391	1,387,897

Table 203 (Continued)
DEATHS, BY STATE, 10 SC, 1930-81
(N)

	State	1940	1941	1942	1943	1944	1945	1946	1947	1948	1949
A.	BAJA CALIF. NORTE	1,288	1,197	1,555	1,681	1,777	1,897	1,909	2,067	2,303	2,588
B.	CHIHUAHUA	11,494	12,032	12,167	12,527	12,369	12,108	12,506	11,106	11,925	11,983
C.	COAHUILA	13,373	12,563	13,660	14,086	12,914	12,132	13,287	10,937	10,827	12,110
D.	NUEVO LEÓN	9,766	9,857	9,583	11,282	10,187	9,657	10,273	9,090	9,316	9,392
E.	SONORA	6,789	6,733	7,340	7,952	7,583	7,739	7,187	6,920	7,503	6,852
F.	TAMAULIPAS	6,462	6,708	7,314	7,621	7,625	6,894	7,560	7,125	7,121	7,940
	Mexico Border	49,172	49,090	51,628	55,149	52,455	50,427	52,722	47,245	48,995	50,865
	Mexico Total	458,906	446,361	471,600	474,950	447,198	433,694	442,935	390,087	407,708	443,559
G.	ARIZONA	5,556	5,452	5,586	5,927	6,205	6,091	5,737	6,032	6,586	6,397
H.	CALIFORNIA	79,742	80,943	84,851	89,109	90,802	92,569	94,678	96,697	98,905	100,354
I.	NEW MEXICO	5,484	5,639	5,203	5,488	5,500	5,520	5,436	5,471	5,609	5,576
J.	TEXAS	62,635	60,581	59,315	62,216	61,565	58,853	59,706	62,662	64,245	63,337
	U.S. Border	153,417	152,615	154,955	162,740	164,072	163,033	165,557	170,862	175,345	175,664
	U.S. Total	1,417,269	1,397,642	1,385,187	1,459,544	1,411,338	1,401,719	1,395,617	1,445,370	1,444,337	1,443,607

Table 203 (Continued)
DEATHS, BY STATE, 10 SC, 1930-81
(N)

	State	1950	1951	1952	1953	1954	1955	1956	1957	1958	1959
A.	BAJA CALIF. NORTE	2,528	2,877	2,888	3,287	3,350	3,510	3,492	3,899	4,033	4,161
B.	CHIHUAHUA	11,204	12,970	12,480	13,677	11,938	11,847	10,782	11,864	13,058	11,382
C.	COAHUILA	10,010	12,604	10,606	12,395	10,112	10,524	8,977	10,917	10,462	9,941
D.	NUEVO LEÓN	8,592	11,094	8,106	10,375	8,399	9,036	7,568	9,055	8,707	9,012
E.	SONORA	6,458	7,765	6,732	7,222	7,121	7,239	6,655	8,013	7,827	7,676
F.	TAMAULIPAS	7,939	9,705	8,117	9,088	8,253	9,284	8,061	9,039	9,657	8,294
	Mexico Border	46,731	57,015	48,929	56,044	49,173	51,440	45,535	52,787	53,744	50,466
	Mexico Total	418,430	458,238	408,823	446,127	378,752	407,522	368,740	414,545	404,529	396,924
G.	ARIZONA	6,422	7,098	7,370	7,750	7,212	7,916	8,464	8,725	9,068	9,602
H.	CALIFORNIA	98,760	104,089	108,552	109,903	109,445	113,847	119,851	124,162	125,924	128,464
I.	NEW MEXICO	5,471	5,614	5,429	5,578	5,373	5,696	5,618	6,114	6,105	6,190
J.	TEXAS	63,349	67,238	64,958	66,271	64,932	65,048	69,665	72,744	73,351	73,563
	U.S. Border	174,002	184,039	186,309	189,502	186,962	192,552	203,598	211,745	214,448	217,819
	U.S. Total	1,452,454	1,482,099	1,496,838	1,517,541	1,481,091	1,528,717	1,564,476	1,633,128	1,647,886	1,656,814

Table 203 (Continued)
DEATHS, BY STATE, 10 SC, 1930-81
(N)

	State	1960	1961	1962	1963	1964	1965	1966	1967	1968	1969
A.	BAJA CALIF. NORTE	4,326	4,033	4,876	5,132	5,637	5,298	5,853	5,566	5,867	6,334
B.	CHIHUAHUA	12,346	13,058	12,822	12,380	13,540	12,178	14,462	12,479	13,342	13,340
C.	COAHUILA	9,734	10,462	10,255	9,256	10,211	8,958	10,566	9,936	10,607	11,066
D.	NUEVO LEÓN	9,066	8,707	9,518	9,494	10,049	9,647	10,306	10,441	11,215	11,302
E.	SONORA	7,939	7,827	8,238	8,174	8,293	7,974	9,105	8,819	8,370	9,278
F.	TAMAULIPAS	8,897	9,657	9,217	9,070	9,697	9,401	9,872	9,986	10,062	9,931
	Mexico Border	52,308	53,744	54,926	53,506	57,427	53,506	60,164	57,227	59,463	61,251
	Mexico Total	402,545	404,529	403,046	412,834	408,275	404,163	424,141	420,298	452,910	458,886
G.	ARIZONA	10,146	10,565	11,177	12,282	12,077	12,357	12,804	13,103	14,021	14,031
H.	CALIFORNIA	135,508	137,327	141,395	145,616	150,955	150,821	157,444	159,610	160,839	166,077
I.	NEW MEXICO	6,525	6,362	6,520	6,876	6,895	6,957	6,970	6,932	7,150	7,209
J.	TEXAS	77,453	76,203	80,752	82,858	82,808	84,142	86,906	86,436	93,908	94,043
	U.S. Border	229,632	230,457	239,844	247,632	252,735	254,277	264,124	266,081	275,918	281,360
	U.S. Total	1,711,982	1,701,522	1,756,720	1,749,677	1,798,051	1,828,136	1,863,149	1,851,323	1,930,082	1,921,990

Table 203 (Continued)

DEATHS, BY STATE, 10 SC, 1930-81

(N)

	State	1970	1971	1972	1973	1974	1975	1976	1977	1978	1979	1980	1981
A.	BAJA CALIF. NORTE	7,012	6,750	6,688	6,856	7,110	6,765	6,743	6,679	5,732	6,806	?	?
B.	CHIHUAHUA	14,201	13,504	14,157	14,243	13,133	12,792	13,396	13,781	13,344	12,838	?	?
C.	COAHUILA	11,602	10,554	11,275	11,459	9,638	9,681	10,151	10,202	8,959	9,294	?	?
D.	NUEVO LEÓN	12,540	12,178	12,866	13,413	12,309	12,065	12,706	12,055	11,016	11,706	?	?
E.	SONORA	9,040	9,590	9,308	9,523	8,997	8,853	9,319	9,456	9,187	9,289	?	?
F.	TAMAULIPAS	10,949	11,024	10,403	10,848	9,888	10,139	10,201	10,772	10,476	10,504	?	?
	Mexico Border	65,344	63,600	64,697	66,342	61,075	60,295	62,516	62,945	58,714	60,437	?	?
	Mexico Total	485,656	458,323	476,206	458,915	433,104	434,515	455,660	450,454	418,381	428,217	?	?
G.	ARIZONA	15,256	20,385	21,609	22,348	17,050	16,980	17,339	18,028	19,198	19,782	21,609	22,348
H.	CALIFORNIA	166,527	169,954	190,247	187,658	170,403	170,687	171,022	170,399	176,069	177,399	190,297	187,658
I.	NEW MEXICO	7,447	8,596	9,080	8,871	8,030	7,977	8,224	8,073	8,456	8,722	9,080	8,871
J.	TEXAS	95,457	107,493	108,586	112,704	99,491	98,471	100,760	100,185	103,845	104,921	108,586	112,704
	U.S. Border	284,687	306,428	329,522	331,581	294,974	294,115	297,345	296,685	307,568	310,824	329,572	331,581
	U.S. Total	1,922,966	1,927,542	1,963,944	1,973,003	1,934,388	1,892,879	1,909,440	1,899,597	1,927,788	1,913,841	1,986,000‡	1,987,000‡

a. Not in registration area.

SOURCE: Mexico: *AEM*, 1938-81, various tables.
United States: *SAUS*, 1930-80; *VSSR*, 1934-37; *VSUS*, 1937-78; *MVSP*, Vol. 30, No. 13 (Dec. 20, 1982) and Vol. 31, No. 6 (Sept. 30, 1981), various tables.

Table 204
MARRIAGES, BY STATE, 10 SC, 1930-81
(N)

	State	1930	1931	1932	1933	1934	1935	1936	1937	1938	1939
A.	BAJA CALIF. NORTE	744	978	1,161	1,296	1,364	1,435	1,453	1,685	1,780	1,918
B.	CHIHUAHUA	3,522	3,532	3,526	4,016	4,793	4,279	5,055	4,996	4,172	4,400
C.	COAHUILA	3,123	3,242	2,996	3,507	3,945	3,899	4,547	4,414	4,285	5,004
D.	NUEVO LEÓN	3,223	3,146	3,546	3,630	4,859	4,566	4,809	5,013	4,573	4,997
E.	SONORA	1,659	1,570	1,724	1,903	2,621	3,005	2,845	2,784	2,616	2,687
F.	TAMAULIPAS	2,721	2,369	2,380	2,643	3,189	2,805	3,243	3,836	3,388	3,665
	Mexico Border	14,992	14,837	15,333	16,995	20,771	19,989	21,952	22,728	20,814	22,671
	Mexico Total	100,724	99,880	95,390	101,745	119,957	118,960	120,288	129,463	123,695	125,979
G.	ARIZONA	7,715	7,575	7,642	~a	~a	~a	~a	~a	12,435	14,585
H.	CALIFORNIA	50,154	47,525	43,164	~a	~a	~a	~a	~a	61,850	57,893
I.	NEW MEXICO	8,711	8,380	8,879	~a	~a	~a	~a	~a	8,559	9,125
J.	TEXAS	45,174	40,512	40,069	~a	~a	~a	~a	~a	75,000	76,800
	U.S. Border	111,754	113,992	99,754	~a	~a	~a	~a	~a	157,844	158,403
	U.S. Total	1,126,856	1,060,554	981,903	~a	~a	~a	~a	~a	1,319,000	1,375,000

Table 204 (Continued)
MARRIAGES, BY STATE, 10 SC, 1930-81
(N)

	State	1940	1941	1942	1943	1944	1945	1946	1947	1948	1949
A.	BAJA CALIF. NORTE	2,802	1,051	1,331	1,011	1,081	1,150	1,464	1,547	1,687	1,962
B.	CHIHUAHUA	5,570	4,585	6,911	7,276	6,538	5,769	6,278	6,590	6,233	6,210
C.	COAHUILA	5,681	4,701	6,973	6,150	6,006	5,713	5,747	5,288	6,325	6,384
D.	NUEVO LEÓN	6,060	4,421	5,524	4,936	4,536	5,073	5,429	4,885	5,129	6,215
E.	SONORA	3,393	2,760	3,662	3,926	3,770	3,659	4,044	4,009	3,684	4,114
F.	TAMAULIPAS	3,740	3,405	4,627	4,200	4,298	4,340	4,544	4,526	4,761	5,493
	Mexico Border	27,246	20,923	29,028	27,499	26,229	25,704	27,506	26,745	27,819	30,378
	Mexico Total	156,358	126,859	176,550	159,845	149,490	151,075	156,971	148,642	155,416	166,133
G.	ARIZONA	23,643[c]	26,700[c]	33,300[c]	21,200[c]	17,083	19,804	27,300[†]	25,600[†]	24,824	23,139
H.	CALIFORNIA	45,069	48,887	76,014	91,808	94,517	102,862	107,995	94,459	88,242	77,961
I.	NEW MEXICO	12,170	~	~	~	11,372	13,652	18,144	14,813	16,492	16,794
J.	TEXAS	86,500	~	~	~	99,506	108,110	143,092[c]	123,798[c]	112,898[c]	96,214[c]
	U.S. Border	167,382	75,587	109,314	113,008	222,478	244,428	296,531	258,670	242,456	214,108
	U.S. Total	1,595,879	1,695,999[b]	1,772,132[b]	1,577,050[b]	1,452,394	1,618,331	2,291,045	1,992,354	1,811,155	1,585,440

Ch. 2, Vital Statistics 23

Table 204 (Continued)

MARRIAGES, BY STATE, 10 SC, 1930-81
(N)

	State	1950	1951	1952	1953	1954	1955	1956	1957	1958	1959
A.	BAJA CALIF. NORTE	2,063	2,214	2,423	2,663	3,154	3,536	3,727	4,351	4,651	4,787
B.	CHIHUAHUA	8,406	6,955	6,508	6,822	8,188	9,137	9,417	8,945	4,651	10,107
C.	COAHUILA	7,313	6,861	7,204	7,188	7,759	7,844	8,125	7,220	9,323	8,562
D.	NUEVO LEÓN	6,601	6,551	7,650	6,804	7,826	8,211	8,368	7,922	7,971	8,887
E.	SONORA	4,326	4,448	4,845	4,739	5,214	5,782	5,775	6,122	6,330	6,251
F.	TAMAULIPAS	6,473	6,272	6,889	6,813	8,579	8,869	8,768	8,050	8,021	8,071
	Mexico Border	35,182	33,301	35,519	35,029	40,720	43,379	44,180	42,610	40,947	46,665
	Mexico Total	177,531	178,165	187,473	183,600	205,771	211,875	222,907	215,292	225,491	238,999
G.	ARIZONA	20,031	20,198	22,436	23,500	20,588	21,831	22,121	9,652	9,917[c]	10,171
H.	CALIFORNIA	79,360	76,748	78,833	79,662	77,947	81,939	87,611	92,607	96,034	101,503
I.	NEW MEXICO	22,717	22,013	22,438	22,511	19,500[c]	22,300[c]	21,600	11,439	5,814[d]	5,657[d]
J.	TEXAS	89,155[c]	88,943	90,270[c]	89,000[c]	89,018	91,210	90,620	89,400	89,821[†]	93,253
	U.S. Border	211,263	207,902	213,977	214,673	207,053	217,280	221,952	203,098	201,586	210,584
	U.S. Total	1,667,231	1,594,694	1,539,318	1,546,000[†]	1,490,000[†]	1,531,000[†]	1,067,939	1,518,000[†]	1,445,000[†]	1,494,000[†]

Table 204 (Continued)

MARRIAGES, BY STATE, 10 SC, 1930-81
(N)

	State	1960	1961	1962	1963	1964	1965	1966	1967	1968	1969
A.	BAJA CALIF. NORTE	4,782	5,321	5,590	5,764	5,811	6,221	6,892	7,031	7,078	7,214
B.	CHIHUAHUA	10,090	10,596	10,982	11,292	11,498	12,700	12,894	13,887	14,285	14,905
C.	COAHUILA	8,378	8,285	8,095	8,125	9,502	10,139	10,097	9,978	10,583	11,858
D.	NUEVO LEÓN	9,243	9,594	9,280	9,530	10,560	11,500	12,560	12,950	14,192	14,697
E.	SONORA	6,161	6,309	6,752	7,066	7,397	7,692	7,959	8,124	8,877	9,282
F.	TAMAULIPAS	7,921	7,845	8,248	8,354	8,666	8,497	9,114	8,888	9,780	10,753
	Mexico Border	46,575	47,950	48,947	50,131	53,434	56,749	59,516	60,858	65,065	68,709
	Mexico Total	239,527	237,069	246,655	257,969	281,389	293,227	307,992	314,263	331,347	347,120
G.	ARIZONA	10,153	10,426	10,745	11,428	12,108	12,113	13,511	14,737	16,758	18,012
H.	CALIFORNIA	105,352	109,642	113,026	121,883	136,131	136,090	144,084	147,378	163,216	166,832
I.	NEW MEXICO	11,051	11,285	5,551	7,997	7,630	13,215[†]	5,926	8,443	7,314[b]	11,109
J.	TEXAS	91,679	96,244	98,699	103,937	110,913	111,542	116,106	124,191	135,528	142,391
	U.S. Border	218,235	227,597	228,021	245,245	266,782	272,950	279,627	294,749	322,816	338,344
	U.S. Total	1,523,381[†]	1,547,945	1,577,360	1,654,003	1,724,697	1,800,207	1,857,294	1,927,023	2,069,258	2,145,438

Table 204 (Continued)

MARRIAGES, BY STATE, 10 SC, 1930-81

(N)

State	1970	1971	1972	1973	1974	1975	1976	1977	1978	1979	1980	1981
A. BAJA CALIF. NORTE	7,880	8,424	9,662	9,575	9,846	8,606	8,690	7,795	7,892	?	?	?
B. CHIHUAHUA	11,971	12,323	15,503	12,750	15,568	14,554	15,849	15,229	15,929	?	?	?
C. COAHUILA	15,023	14,653	19,065	16,436	17,150	16,725	14,307	13,830	12,812	?	?	?
D. NUEVO LEÓN	15,249	15,947	20,475	18,815	21,680	19,531	19,298	20,488	20,644	?	?	?
E. SONORA	9,916	10,165	14,937	11,748	12,847	12,106	11,586	11,110	10,764	?	?	?
F. TAMAULIPAS	11,282	11,267	21,065	12,362	16,174	14,066	14,860	13,858	13,469	?	?	?
Mexico Border	71,321	72,779	100,707	81,686	93,265	85,588	84,590	82,310	81,510	?	?	?
Mexico Total	356,658	378,222	622,064	452,640	505,544	472,091	482,810	466,788	463,157			
G. ARIZONA	18,508	20,865	23,318	26,180	27,038	26,558	26,534	26,955	27,725	29,603	30,230	31,784
H. CALIFORNIA	172,388	168,049	175,924	169,320	160,887	154,812	151,284	149,461	188,056	199,698	218,404	214,708
I. NEW MEXICO	12,422	14,008	14,167	15,178	15,886	15,790	15,616	16,385	16,582	16,309	16,324	17,130
J. TEXAS	139,491	140,232	149,009	152,162	153,002	153,154	157,320	159,576	167,827	172,757	187,118	192,368
U.S. Border	342,809	343,154	362,418	362,840	356,813	350,314	350,754	352,332	400,190	418,367	452,076	455,990
U.S. Total	2,158,802	2,190,481	2,282,154	2,284,108	2,229,667	2,152,662	2,154,807	2,178,367	2,282,272	2,331,337	2,413,000[‡]	2,438,000[‡]

a. U.S. marriage data not collected 1933-38.
b. Includes estimates for states not reported separately.
c. Licenses issued.
d. Incomplete data.

SOURCE: Mexico: *AEM*, 1938-81, various tables.
United States: *SAUS*, 1930-80; *VSSR*, 1934-37; *VSUS*, 1937-78; *MVSR*, Vol. 30, No. 13 (Dec. 20, 1982), and Vol. 30, No. 4 (July 31, 1981).

Table 205

DIVORCES, BY STATE, 10 SC, 1930-81

(N)

	State	1930	1931	1932	1933	1934	1935	1936	1937	1938	1939
A.	BAJA CALIF. NORTE	17	16	18	24	40	56	46	42	?	?
B.	CHIHUAHUA	126	123	665	1,475	2,223	1,849	1,457	1,291	?	?
C.	COAHUILA	45	58	59	59	56	138	167	188	?	?
D.	NUEVO LEÓN	51	57	45	43	49	62	80	79	?	?
E.	SONORA	180	107	132	99	121	102	107	96	?	?
F.	TAMAULIPAS	34	47	57	56	43	266	201	236	?	?
	Mexico Border	453	408	976	1,756	2,532	2,473	2,058	1,932	?	?
	Mexico Total	1,626	1,606	2,346	3,472	4,535	4,752	4,732	4,472		4,539
G.	ARIZONA	1,136	1,125	848	?	?	?	?	?	1,655	1,738
H.	CALIFORNIA	15,603	15,113	14,097	?	?	?	?	?	23,700	23,800
I.	NEW MEXICO	770	725	696	?	?	?	?	?	1,000	1,200
J.	TEXAS	16,645	15,788	14,172	?	?	?	?	?	25,300	26,100
	U.S. Border	34,154	32,751	29,813	?	?	?	?	?	51,655	52,838
	U.S. Total	191,591	183,664	160,338	359,000					244,000	251,000

Table 205 (Continued)

DIVORCES, BY STATE, 10 SC, 1930-81

(N)

	State	1940	1941	1942	1943	1944	1945	1946	1947	1948	1949
A.	BAJA CALIF. NORTE	72	69	87	97	92	74	73	87	94	101
B.	CHIHUAHUA	933	1,067	1,732	3,160	4,154	3,919	3,693	2,744	1,808	1,640
C.	COAHUILA	189	261	350	360	376	338	316	330	318	322
D.	NUEVO LEÓN	73	90	85	109	137	127	127	94	154	140
E.	SONORA	101	110	139	166	219	231	250	281	230	202
F.	TAMAULIPAS	222	284	452	479	537	441	488	532	455	503
	Mexico Border	1,590	1,881	2,845	4,371	5,515	5,130	4,947	4,068	3,059	2,749
	Mexico Total	4,291	5,179	6,604	7,972	9,297	9,602	9,950	8,693	6,882	6,777
G.	ARIZONA	1,913	?	?	?	?	2,500†	2,900†	2,400	?	4,478
H.	CALIFORNIA	24,200†	?	?	?	?	?	52,300†	?	42,342	38,440
I.	NEW MEXICO	1,200†	?	?	?	?	3,124	3,898	3,160	2,631	2,884
J.	TEXAS	27,500†	28,400	32,200	38,100	39,900	49,345	57,112	43,584	39,587	38,027
	U.S. Border	54,813†	?	?	?	?	54,969†	116,210†	49,144	84,560†	83,829†
	U.S. Total	264,000†	293,000	321,000	359,000	400,000	485,000†	610,000	483,000	408,000†	397,000†

Table 205 (Continued)

DIVORCES, BY STATE, 10 SC, 1930-81

(N)

	State	1950	1951	1952	1953	1954	1955	1956	1957	1958	1959
A.	BAJA CALIF. NORTE	112	121	135	138	156	170	214	231	281	356
B.	CHIHUAHUA	2,232	2,226	2,738	3,104	4,039	5,606	6,599	6,599	6,769	8,201
C.	COAHUILA	353	364	318	455	551	557	611	592	575	650
D.	NUEVO LEÓN	173	199	204	311	442	443	436	413	418	436
E.	SONORA	204	208	222	216	218	268	294	287	304	316
F.	TAMAULIPAS	469	527	664	665	671	764	769	812	773	733
	Mexico Border	3,543	3,645	4,281	4,889	6,077	7,808	8,923	8,934	9,120	10,692
	Mexico Total	7,929	7,803	8,533	8,914	10,418	12,208	12,418	13,436	13,451	15,455
G.	ARIZONA	4,062	4,240	4,905	5,125	4,790[†]	3,526	5,571	5,328	5,910[†]	6,503[†]
H.	CALIFORNIA	38,833	38,542	41,398	40,196	42,093	41,599	42,471	43,999	43,700	47,572[a]
I.	NEW MEXICO	2,655	2,942	2,940	~	2,500[†]	2,140	2,337[†]	3,065[†]	2,771[a]	2,093[a]
J.	TEXAS	37,400[†]	37,330[a]	37,300[†]	39,000[†]	36,000[a]	34,921[a]	33,831[a]	34,871[a]	33,678[a]	35,623
	U.S. Border	82,950	83,054	86,543	84,321	85,383	82,166	84,210	87,263	86,059	91,791
	U.S. Total	385,144[†]	381,000[†]	392,000[†]	390,000[†]	379,000[†]	377,000[†]	382,000[†]	381,000[†]	368,000[†]	395,000[†]

Table 205 (Continued)

DIVORCES, BY STATE, 10 SC, 1930-81

(N)

	State	1960	1961	1962	1963	1964	1965	1966	1967	1968	1969
A.	BAJA CALIF. NORTE	427	434	495	519	537	563	677	760	747	815
B.	CHIHUAHUA	7,669	9,291	10,797	12,187	12,349	16,475	20,173	24,074	16,551	21,085
C.	COAHUILA	545	507	519	501	632	688	676	708	724	783
D.	NUEVO LEÓN	452	417	384	428	484	536	566	573	470	543
E.	SONORA	355	395	381	347	342	411	386	398	474	430
F.	TAMAULIPAS	676	603	326	328	390	409	464	448	420	491
	Mexico Border	10,124	11,647	12,902	14,310	14,734	19,082	22,942	26,961	19,386	24,147
	Mexico Total	14,964	16,528	17,459	19,277	20,161	24,705	28,623	32,907	25,623	30,504
G.	ARIZONA	4,780	6,973	7,788	8,482	8,790	8,575	9,186[†]	10,142	10,701	11,918
H.	CALIFORNIA	49,276	51,644	54,011	56,274	59,094	69,926[a]	69,127	69,846	75,416	81,546
I.	NEW MEXICO	2,811[a]	3,220[a]	3,645	3,470	3,280[a]	3,662[a]	3,054[†]	1,545[a]	2,585[a]	3,539
J.	TEXAS	34,732[a]	35,340[a]	36,918	39,219	40,842	41,323	43,046	45,339	48,852	46,918
	U.S. Border	91,599	97,177	102,362	107,445	112,006	123,486	116,145	126,872	137,554	143,921
	U.S. Total	393,000[†]	414,000[†]	413,000[†]	428,000[†]	450,000[†]	479,000[†]	499,000[†]	523,000[†]	584,000[†]	639,000[†]

Table 205 (Continued)
DIVORCES, BY STATE, 10 SC, 1930-81
(N)

	State	1970	1971	1972	1973	1974	1975	1976	1977	1978	1979	1980	1981
A.	BAJA CALIF. NORTE	771	736	951	985	916	1,006	1,006	1,146	1,088	1,218	?	?
B.	CHIHUAHUA	21,500	705	673	710	746	760	1,136	1,294	1,431	1,613	?	?
C.	COAHUILA	846	2,592	570	699	199	953	897	957	823	919	?	?
D.	NUEVO LEÓN	574	531	646	701	967	1,095	1,256	1,232	1,336	992	?	?
E.	SONORA	455	464	452	611	671	450	595	459	445	589	?	?
F.	TAMAULIPAS	474	534	544	582	601	705	725	811	857	849	?	?
	Mexico Border	24,620	5,562	3,836	4,288	4,100	4,969	5,615	5,899	5,980	6,180	?	?
	Mexico Toral	31,181	1,215	11,954	13,517	13,594	16,791	19,002	21,269	21,394	22,849	?	?
G.	ARIZONA	12,714	14,588	13,197	14,036	16,936	17,577	19,029	16,578	17,320	19,982	19,921	20,988
H.	CALIFORNIA	112,942	68,309	110,718	117,509	121,714	128,492	133,024	132,193	132,850	137,683	134,309	134,371
I.	NEW MEXICO	4,375[a]	4,580[a]	5,251[a]	5,383	7,863	8,413	9,118	9,143	9,608	9,978	10,444	10,592
J.	TEXAS	51,530	55,568	60,343	64,152	69,762	76,685	79,905	82,265	85,784	92,399	97,161	99,021
	U.S. Border	181,561	143,045	189,509	201,080	216,275	231,167	241,076	240,179	245,562	260,042	261,835	264,972
	U.S. Total	708,000[†]	773,000[†]	845,000[†]	915,000[†]	977,000[†]	1,036,000[†]	1,083,000[†]	1,091,000[†]	1,130,000[†]	1,181,000[†]	1,182,000[†]	1,219,000[‡]

a. Incomplete data.

SOURCE: Mexico: *AEM*, 1938-81, various tables.
United States: *SAUS*, 1930-81; *VSSR*, 1934-37; *VSUS*, 1937-78; *MVSR*, Vol. 30,
No. 13 (Dec. 20, 1982), and Vol. 30, No. 2 (May 29, 1981), various tables.

3
Religion

Table 300

MEXICAN POPULATION, BY RELIGION, 6 SC, 1900–70

(N)

State and Category	1900	1910	1920	1930	1940	1950	1960	1970
A. BAJA CALIF. NORTE								
Total Population	7,583	9,760	23,537	48,327	78,907	226,965	520,165	870,421
Catholic	~a	~a	~a	39,798	71,919	219,798	490,719	830,433
Protestant	~a	~a	~a	1,099	1,468	4,351	12,450	20,406
Jewish	~a	~a	~a	20	37	128	1,659	399
Other	~a	~a	~a	3,383	1,300	2,688	4,338	5,179
No Religion	~a	~a	~a	4,027	4,183	~	5,241	14,004
Unknown	~a	~a	~a	~	~	~	5,758	~
B. CHIHUAHUA								
Total Population	327,784	405,707	401,622	491,792	623,944	846,414	1,226,793	1,612,525
Catholic	314,804	384,993	394,155	468,367	595,417	816,984	1,151,351	1,535,563
Protestant	2,374	4,592	4,023	4,951	7,042	13,572	26,481	41,811
Jewish	~	~	~	127	164	118	2,197	575
Other	1,266	1,059	99	10,471	10,458	15,470	18,072	7,780
No Religion	8,434	9,294	1,102	7,861	10,781	~	5,823	26,796
Unknown	906	5,769	2,243	15	82	~	22,869	~
C. COAHUILA								
Total Population	296,938	362,092	393,480	436,425	550,717	720,619	907,734	1,114,956
Catholic	293,490	353,490	386,173	421,297	530,137	702,761	866,547	1,073,660
Protestant	3,346	6,289	4,542	9,136	11,119	15,580	22,514	25,255
Jewish	~	~	~	116	269	105	1,357	340
Other	61	1,012	333	1,132	968	2,173	3,687	3,879
No Religion	~	317	465	4,739	8,211	~	4,316	11,822
Unknown	41	984	1,967	8	13	~	9,313	~
D. NUEVO LEÓN								
Total Population	327,937	365,150	336,412	417,491	541,147	740,191	1,078,848	1,694,689
Catholic	324,438	359,855	329,301	406,660	519,596	720,915	1,037,830	1,619,288
Protestant	3,062	4,498	4,163	7,455	10,220	16,679	25,747	47,714
Jewish	~	~	~	214	342	288	3,904	867
Other	48	173	506	564	500	2,309	5,725	6,278
No Religion	130	61	1,501	2,546	10,487	~	4,624	20,542
Unknown	259	563	941	52	2	~	1,018	~
E. SONORA								
Total Population	221,682	265,383	275,127	316,271	364,176	510,607	783,378	1,098,720
Catholic	218,096	255,703	262,059	306,717	355,645	502,657	758,234	1,061,138
Protestant	1,913	3,419	2,344	3,369	2,901	6,693	12,616	16,188
Jewish	~	~	~	73	19	37	1,971	332
Other	1,215	5,568	1,315	2,115	259	1,220	3,005	3,185
No Religion	20	39	5,955	3,996	5,348	~	4,555	17,877
Unknown	438	654	3,454	1	4	~	2,997	~
F. TAMAULIPAS								
Total Population	218,948	249,641	286,904	344,039	458,832	718,167	1,024,182	1,456,858
Catholic	215,866	246,198	267,609	323,298	428,637	694,740	970,999	1,384,906
Protestant	2,359	2,697	5,609	8,221	11,866	20,222	34,336	41,911
Jewish	~	~	~	212	176	146	3,574	578
Other	20	162	1,629	1,911	1,069	3,050	6,738	5,891
No Religion	12	39	4,999	10,387	17,083	~	7,269	23,572
Unknown	691	545	7,058	10	1	~	1,266	~

Table 300 (Continued)

MEXICAN POPULATION, BY RELIGION, 6 SC, 1900-70

(N)

State and Category	1900	1910	1920	1930	1940	1950	1960	1970
MEXICAN BORDER								
Total Population	1,400,872	1,657,733	1,717,082	2,054,345	2,617,723	3,762,963	5,541,100	7,848,169
Catholic	1,366,694	1,600,239	1,639,297	1,966,137	2,501,351	3,657,855	5,275,680	7,504,988
Protestant	13,054	21,495	20,681	34,231	44,616	77,097	124,144	193,285
Jewish	~	~	~	762	1,007	822	14,662	3,091
Other	2,610	7,974	3,882	19,576	14,554	27,180	41,565	32,192
No Religion	9,196	9,750	14,022	33,556	56,093	~	31,828	114,613
Unknown	2,435	8,515	15,663	83	102	~	43,221	~
MEXICO TOTAL								
Total Population	13,607,259	15,160,369	14,334,780	16,552,722	19,653,552	25,791,017	34,923,129	48,225,238
Catholic	13,519,655	15,033,176	13,921,226	16,179,667	18,977,585	25,329,498	33,692,503	46,380,401
Protestant	51,796	68,838	73,951	130,322	177,954	330,111	578,515	876,879
Jewish	~	~	~	9,072	14,167	17,574	100,750	49,181
Other	3,816	13,342	22,718	56,696	35,758	113,834	137,208	150,329
No Religion	21,166	20,014	208,836	175,180	443,671	~	192,963	758,448
Unknown	18,635	24,999	108,049	1,785	4,417	~	221,190	~

a. No separate statistics for Baja California Norte until 1930; earlier years combined north and south territories.

SOURCE: *CGP*, 1900-70.

Table 301

MEXICAN POPULATION WITHOUT RELIGIOUS AFFILIATION[1], 6 SC, 1900-70

(%)

State	1900	1910	1920	1930	1940	1950	1960	1970
A. BAJA CALIF. NORTE	~	~	~	8.33	5.30	~	1.00	1.61
B. CHIHUAHUA	2.57	2.29	.27	1.60	1.73	~	.47	1.66
C. COAHUILA	~	.09	.12	1.09	1.49	~	.48	1.06
D. NUEVO LEÓN	.04	.02	.45	.61	1.94	~	.43	1.21
E. SONORA	.01	.01	2.16	1.26	1.47	~	.58	1.63
F. TAMAULIPAS	.01	.02	1.74	3.02	3.72	~	.71	1.62
Mexico Border	.66	.59	.82	1.63	2.14	~	.57	1.46
Mexico Total	.15	.13	1.46	1.06	2.26	~	.55	1.59

1. Persons claiming "no religion" on census.

SOURCE: Calculated from *CGP*, 1900-1970.

Table 302
U.S. CATHOLIC POPULATION, 4 SC, 1960–80

State	1960 N	1960 % of Total Population	1970 N	1970 % of Total Population	1980 N	1980 % of Total Population
G. ARIZONA	276,000	21.2	336,356	19.0	467,710	17.2
H. CALIFORNIA	3,277,400	20.9	4,053,881	20.3	4,844,744	20.5
I. NEW MEXICO	329,511	34.6	341,224	33.6	372,456	28.6
J. TEXAS	1,848,176	19.3	1,997,122	17.8	2,375,160	16.7
U.S. Border	5,731,087	20.8	6,728,583	19.2	8,060,070	19.2
U.S. Total	40,871,302	22.9	47,872,089	23.6	49,812,178	22.0

SOURCE: *The Official Catholic Directory*, 1960–80.

Table 303
U.S. JEWISH POPULATION†, 4 SC, 1960–80

State	1960 N	1960 % of Total Population	1970 N	1970 % of Total Population	1980 N	1980 % of Total Population
G. ARIZONA	14,800	1.1	21,000	1.1	41,285	1.7
H. CALIFORNIA	530,300	3.4	721,045	3.6	753,945	3.3
I. NEW MEXICO	2,700	.3	2,700	.3	7,155	.6
J. TEXAS	60,900	.6	67,505	.6	72,545	.5
U.S. Border	608,700	2.2	812,250	2.4	874,930	2.1
U.S. Total	5,531,500	3.1	6,059,730	2.9	5,920,890	2.7

SOURCE: *American Jewish Yearbook*, 1961–81.

4
Immigration

Table 400
MEXICAN IMMIGRATION[1] TO THE UNITED STATES, 1930–79

Year	Mexican Immigrants (N)	As % of Western Hemisphere Immigrants to U.S.	As % of Total Immigrants to U.S.
1930	12,703	14.4	5.3
1931	3,333	10.8	3.4
1932	2,171	17.3	6.1
1933	1,936	19.5	8.4
1934	1,801	15.8	6.1
1935	1,560	14.0	4.5
1936	1,716	14.6	4.7
1937	2,347	13.4	4.7
1938	2,502	12.2	3.7
1939	2,640	15.4	3.2
1940	2,313	13.0	3.3
1941	2,824	12.6	5.5
1942	2,378	14.5	8.3
1943	4,172	32.0	17.6
1944	6,598	28.6	23.1
1945	6,702	22.6	17.6
1946	7,146	15.5	6.6
1947	7,558	14.3	5.1
1948	8,384	15.9	4.9
1949	8,083	16.4	4.3
1950	6,744	15.3	2.7
1951	6,153	13.0	3.0
1952	9,079	14.9	3.4
1953	17,183	22.1	10.1
1954	30,645	32.1	14.7
1955	43,702	39.6	18.4
1956	61,320	42.4	19.1
1957	49,321	36.8	15.1
1958	26,791	23.7	10.6
1959	22,909	24.6	8.8
1960	32,708	27.4	12.3
1961	41,476	29.7	15.3
1962	55,805	35.8	19.7
1963	55,986	32.9	18.3
1964	34,448	21.7	11.8
1965	40,686	23.8	13.7
1966	47,217	29.0	14.6
1967	43,034	25.3	11.9
1968	44,716	17.0	9.8
1969	45,748	27.9	12 8
1970	44,821	27.7	12.0
1971	50,324	29.3	13.6
1972	64,209	37.1	16.7
1973	70,411	39.2	17.6
1974	71,863	40.2	18.2
1975	62,552	35.8	16.2
1976	74,449	34.9	14.8
1977	44,646	20.0	9.7
1978	92,681	34.8	15.4
1979	52,479	26.6	11.4

1. Mexican immigrants are defined as nonresident aliens (i.e., non-U.S. citizens) having Mexico as country of last permanent residence and admitted to the United States for permanent residence.

SOURCE: Calculated from *HSUS*, 1975, vol. I, series C89-119; *INS-AR*, 1971-77; *INS, Statistical Yearbook*, 1978-79.

Table 401
U.S. IMMIGRATION TO MEXICO, 1930–73

Year	U.S. Immigrants (N)	As % of Western Hemisphere Immigrants	As % of Total Immigrants
1930	7,561	89.8	48.4
1931	5,014	92.0	52.1
1932	604	91.5	35.8
1933	39	61.9	5.4
1934	112	46.5	13.7
1935	115	79.9	16.5
1936	180	62.3	18.3
1937	261	53.2	25.3
1938	145	45.2	20.5
1939	~	~	~
1940	152	51.0	5.9
1941	216	56.1	8.5
1942	302	58.6	8.9
1943	469	63.3	26.1
1944	612	61.7	26.4
1945	611	65.0	37.2
1946	1,349	74.2	34.9
1947	1,321	79.5	26.9
1948	1,198	60.8	34.1
1949	937	72.7	38.3
1950	1,056	65.6	39.2
1951	1,132	72.1	38.6
1952	1,157	64.8	38.9
1953	1,045	66.5	38.4
1954	1,251	70.4	40.1
1955	1,244	63.0	34.0
1956	1,314	60.6	40.1
1957	1,538	56.0	29.3
1958	1,339	54.1	27.5
1959	1,308	53.0	34.2
1960	1,190	49.2	33.5
1961	649	78.1	39.1
1962	727	76.4	40.9
1963	931	77.3	46.1
1964	1,178	85.0	55.3
1965	1,012	82.1	47.0
1966	1,193	84.3	49.2
1967	997	80.4	43.5
1968	938	81.8	43.8
1969	876	78.5	38.4
1970	845	72.7	37.0
1971	914	80.3	43.8
1972	882	73.7	41.2
1973	862	77.3	40.4

SOURCE: Calculated from *AEM*, 1938-78, various tables.

Table 402

MEXICAN WORKERS DEPARTING TO AND RETURNING FROM THE UNITED STATES, 6 SC, 1942–67[a]

(N)

	State	1942 Departing	1942 Returning	1943 Departing	1943 Returning	1944 Departing	1944 Returning	1945 Departing	1945 Returning	1946 Departing	1946 Returning
A.	BAJA CALIF. NORTE	2	0	24	4	18	10	6	0	1	0
B.	CHIHUAHUA	8	0	142	25	1,179	149	2,110	779	6,230	1,728
C.	COAHUILA	8	2	277	66	212	201	1,347	578	1,441	1,079
D.	NUEVO LEÓN	6	2	103	29	140	92	38	45	6	27
E.	SONORA	3	0	79	8	28	14	9	7	5	6
F.	TAMAULIPAS	11	4	186	52	1,267	329	3,076	1,401	3	675
	Mexico Border	38	8	811	184	2,844	795	6,586	2,810	7,686	3,515
	Mexico Total	4,142	903	75,923	42,368	118,059	64,257	104,641	79,190	31,190	37,597

	State	1947 Departing	1947 Returning	1948 Departing	1948 Returning	1949 Departing	1949 Returning	1950 Departing	1950 Returning	1951 Departing	1951 Returning
A.	BAJA CALIF. NORTE	2,381	7	1	61	32	8	25	2	419	6
B.	CHIHUAHUA	9,447	1,573	45	6,279	3,808	3,949	104	1,069	55,002	24
C.	COAHUILA	4,030	364	349	916	717	1,724	4,671	301	14,425	192
D.	NUEVO LEÓN	4,186	22	1,824	447	414	853	1,040	66	7,872	308
E.	SONORA	1,340	4	6	21	2,587	2,576	666	289	4,884	664
F.	TAMAULIPAS	2,846	14	2,205	850	92	630	512	29	4,629	109
	Mexico Border	24,230	1,984	4,430	8,574	7,650	9,740	7,018	1,756	87,231	1,303
	Mexico Total	72,769	27,796	24,320	18,789	19,866	27,880	23,399	5,034	308,878	6,510

	State	1952 Departing	1952 Returning	1953 Departing	1953 Returning	1954 Departing	1954 Returning	1955 Departing	1955 Returning	1956 Departing	1956 Returning
A.	BAJA CALIF. NORTE	10	3	13	0	46	0	713	0	3,621	0
B.	CHIHUAHUA	35,984	5	54,392	23	43,939	4	31,142	0	29,965	0
C.	COAHUILA	6,449	14	11,889	15	9,500	6	19,612	0	21,771	0
D.	NUEVO LEÓN	1,799	49	717	11	6,261	33	21,987	0	23,217	0
E.	SONORA	73	81	16	4	414	3	1,803	0	1,692	0
F.	TAMAULIPAS	628	17	392	17	2,805	13	5,605	0	8,269	0
	Mexico Border	44,943	169	67,419	70	62,919	59	80,862	0	88,535	0
	Mexico Total	195,963	7,187	130,794	5,511	153,975	2,196	398,703	0	432,926	424,677

Table 402 (Continued)

MEXICAN WORKERS DEPARTING TO AND RETURNING FROM THE UNITED STATES, 6 SC, 1942-67[a]

(N)

	State	1957 Departing	1957 Returning	1958 Departing	1958 Returning	1959 Departing	1959 Returning	1960 Departing	1960 Returning	1961 Departing	1961 Returning
A.	BAJA CALIF. NORTE	3,125	0	2,252	0	6,746	0	277	0	202	0
B.	CHIHUAHUA	28,092	0	37,402	0	35,509	0	32,897	0	32,800	0
C.	COAHUILA	22,629	0	24,160	0	18,818	0	11,887	0	13,760	0
D.	NUEVO LEÓN	17,963	0	23,285	0	25,637	0	21,631	0	12,483	0
E.	SONORA	2,418	0	3,114	0	6,789	0	6,967	0	5,159	0
F.	TAMAULIPAS	6,076	0	8,200	0	7,631	0	7,473	0	9,811	0
	Mexico Border	80,303	0	98,413	0	101,130	0	81,132	0	74,215	0
	Mexico Total	436,049	405,215	432,491	436,353	444,408	426,536	319,412	325,999	296,464	292,520

	State	1962 Departing	1962 Returning	1963 Departing	1963 Returning	1964 Departing	1964 Returning	1965 Departing	1965 Returning	1966 Departing	1966 Returning	1967 Departing	1967 Returning
A.	BAJA CALIF. NORTE	419	?	139	?	331	?	1,000	?	1,633	?	?	?
B.	CHIHUAHUA	10,765	?	15,111	?	12,769	?	?	?	?	?	?	?
C.	COAHUILA	6,194	?	7,406	?	4,376	?	1,000	?	?	?	?	?
D.	NUEVO LEÓN	6,339	?	5,105	?	3,967	?	?	?	?	?	?	?
E.	SONORA	3,662	?	2,989	?	2,780	?	600	?	?	?	?	?
F.	TAMAULIPAS	567	?	2,329	?	1,424	?	?	?	?	?	?	?
	Mexico Border	27,946	?	33,079	?	25,647	?	2,600	?	1,633	?	6,000	?
	Mexico Total	198,522	217,761	189,528	?	179,298	?	19,970	?	6,133	?	?	?

a. Data from 1942-64 relate to the Bracero program, arranged for the temporary transfer of Mexican workers to the United States.

SOURCE: Adapted from Moisés González Navarro, *Población y sociedad en México (1900-1970)*, vol. 2, table 41; and *AEM*, 1964/65, and 1966/67, tables 3.29 and 3.31, respectively.

Table 403

UNDOCUMENTED MEXICAN WORKERS IN THE UNITED STATES, 1970-81[a]

Category	1970	1971	1972	1973	1974	1975	1976	1977	1978	1979	1980	1981
Mexican Undocumented Workers Apprehended and Considered "Deportable"[1]	219,254	290,152	355,099	480,588	616,630	579,448	848,130	792,613	841,525	866,761	734,219	797,923
Working in Agriculture	53,674	74,423	84,084	101,220	111,289	116,250	140,260	103,300	96,297	102,817	51,035	75,241
Working in Trades, Crafts, and Industry	13,625	15,895	21,217	24,996	26,555	24,413	29,001	24,393	30,989	30,879	16,772	23,730
Other	151,955	199,834	249,798	354,372	478,786	438,785	678,869	664,920	714,239	733,065	666,412	698,952
Mexicans as % of Total Undocumented Workers Apprehended	94.9	95.9	96.1	96.5	97.1	97.0	96.6	97.5	97.6	97.5	96.7	96.7

1. Only includes undocumenteds apprehended by Border Patrol.

a. 1970-75, year ended June 30; 1976-81, year ended Sept. 30.

SOURCE: *INS-AR*, 1970-81.

Table 404

U.S. IMMIGRATION AND NATURALIZATION SERVICE MAN-HOURS PER DEPORTABLE UNDOCUMENTEDS LOCATED, 1978-82[a]

(N)

Year	Border Patrol[1]		Investigations[2]	
	Mexican Undocumenteds	All Undocumenteds	Mexican Undocumenteds	All Undocumenteds
1978	7.03	6.86	21.38	15.58
1979	7.22	7.04	22.17	16.20
1980	8.26	7.99	33.70	19.53
1981	7.94	7.68	34.62	20.60
1982	8.12	7.88	25.48	16.44

1. Includes line watch, patrol, farm-ranch check, traffic check, city patrol, boat patrol, crewman-stowaway, aircraft operations, liaison, intelligence, litigation, identification, special programs, and headquarters staff sections.
2. Includes subversive, criminal, fraud, general, and area control sections.

a. Productive and support hours divided by number of undocumenteds located inside the United States.

SOURCE: INS forms G-23.18 (Monthly Report of Deportable Aliens Found in the U.S.) and G-23.21 (Report of Field Operations), 1978-81.

Table 405

MEXICAN UNDOCUMENTEDS COUNTED[†] IN THE 1980 U.S. CENSUS, BY PERIOD OF ENTRY, 1960–80[a]

Period of Entry	Mexican Undocumenteds (T)	As % of Western Hemisphere Undocumenteds in U.S.	As % of Total Undocumenteds in U.S.
Total Entered Since 1960[1]	931	64.1	45.5
Entered 1960–69	138	42.3	24.2
Entered 1970–74	280	64.7	50.8
Entered 1974–80	292	72.3	53.5

1. Includes 36,000 Mexican undocumenteds who entered before 1960 (only figure available for pre-1960 undocumenteds).

a. Estimates based on differences between 1980 census alien population as modified and 1980 alien registration (I-53) data adjusted for underregistration.

SOURCE: Jeffrey S. Passel and Robert Warren, "Estimates of Illegal Aliens from Mexico Counted in the 1980 United States Census," paper presented at annual meeting of Population Association of America, Pittsburg, Penn., April 14-16, 1983.

5
Employment, Wages, and Prices

Table 500

ECONOMICALLY ACTIVE POPULATION, EMPLOYMENT, AND UNEMPLOYMENT IN MEXICAN BORDER CITIES, 1960-70

State and City	1960				1970			
	EAP (N)	Employed (N)	Unemployed (N)	Unemployment Rate (%)	EAP (N)	Employed (N)	Unemployed (N)	Unemployment Rate (%)
A. BAJA CALIF. NORTE								
Ensenada	21,999	20,881	1,118	5.1	29,187	27,965	1,222	4.2
Mexicali	90,376	84,706	5,670	6.3	99,381	94,087	5,294	5.3
Tijuana	52,832	50,491	2,341	4.4	88,816	84,803	4,013	4.5
B. CHIHUAHUA								
Ciudad Juárez	85,989	83,029	2,960	3.4	107,384	101,338	6,046	5.6
F. TAMAULIPAS								
Matamoros	45,882	44,816	1,066	2.3	49,738	47,121	2,617	5.3
Nuevo Laredo	30,576	29,660	916	3.0	39,659	38,205	1,454	3.7
Reynosa	44,925	44,198	727	1.6	37,242	35,874	1,368	3.7

SOURCE: *LFN*, table III-5.

Table 501

ECONOMICALLY ACTIVE POPULATION[1] IN MEXICAN BORDER CITIES, BY SECTOR, 1970 AND 1975

		1970		1975	
	State and City	N	% of Total	N	% of Total
A.	**BAJA CALIF. NORTE**				
	Mexicali				
	Total EAP	98,738	100.0	120,835	100.0
	Primary Activities[2]	32,820	33.2	40,166	33.2
	Petroleum Industry	116	.1	145	.1
	Mining	318	.3	386	.3
	Manufacturing	15,193	15.4	18,596	15.4
	Construction	4,329	4.4	5,293	4.4
	Electrical Energy	542	.5	665	.6
	Commerce	12,469	12.6	15,261	12.6
	Transportation	2,713	2.7	3,323	2.8
	Services	3,822	3.9	4,676	3.9
	Government	~	~	~	~
	Unclassified	6,719	6.8	8,217	6.8
	Tijuana				
	Total EAP	89,013	100.0	~	100.0
	Primary Activities[2]	8,176	9.2	~	~
	Petroleum Industry	164	.2	~	~
	Mining	277	.3	~	~
	Manufacturing	18,936	21.3	~	~
	Construction	6,386	7.2	~	~
	Electrical Energy	469	.5	~	~
	Commerce	15,069	16.9	~	~
	Transportation	2,924	3.3	~	~
	Services	25,923	29.1	~	~
	Government	2,772	3.1	~	~
	Unclassified	7,917	8.9	~	~
B.	**CHIHUAHUA**				
	Ciudad Juárez				
	Total EAP	108,078	100.0	144,051	100.0
	Primary Activities[2]	9,342	8.6	12,446	8.6
	Petroleum Industry	198	.2	274	.2
	Mining	403	.4	533	.4
	Manufacturing	19,215	17.8	25,612	17.8
	Construction	8,851	8.2	11,798	8.2
	Electrical Energy	419	.4	562	.4
	Commerce	19,149	17.7	25,526	17.7
	Transportation	4,532	4.2	6,036	4.2
	Government	3,522	3.3	4,696	3.3
	Unclassified	8,823	8.2	11,755	8.2
C.	**COAHUILA**				
	Ciudad Acuña				
	Total EAP	9,299	100.0	11,619	100.0
	Primary Activities[2]	1,915	20.6	2,393	20.6
	Petroleum Industry	9	.1	10	.1
	Mining	273	2.9	342	2.9
	Manufacturing	1,239	13.3	1,549	13.3
	Construction	828	8.9	1,035	8.9
	Electrical Energy	26	.3	33	.3
	Commerce	1,286	13.8	1,607	13.8
	Transportation	277	3.0	346	3.0
	Services	2,508	27.0	3,134	27.0
	Government	402	4.3	502	4.3
	Unclassified	536	5.8	669	5.8

Table 501 (Continued)

ECONOMICALLY ACTIVE POPULATION[1] IN MEXICAN BORDER CITIES, BY SECTOR, 1970 AND 1975

State and City	1970		1975	
	N	% of Total	N	% of Total
Piedras Negras				
Total EAP	12,130	100.0	20,922	100.0
Primary Activities[2]	1,957	16.1	3,375	16.1
Petroleum Industry	8	.1	15	.1
Mining	113	.9	195	.9
Manufacturing	2,792	23.0	4,816	23.0
Construction	748	6.2	1,291	6.2
Electrical Energy	50	.4	86	.4
Commerce	1,630	13.4	2,812	13.4
Transportation	434	3.6	749	3.6
Services	2,959	24.4	5,103	24.4
Government	485	4.0	837	4.0
Unclassified	954	7.9	1,644	7.9
E. SONORA				
Nogales				
Total EAP	14,218	100.0	17,080	100.0
Primary Activities[2]	1,017	7.2	1,221	7.1
Petroleum Industry	12	.1	15	.1
Mining	77	.5	92	.5
Manufacturing	2,653	18.7	3,187	18.7
Construction	999	7.0	1,201	7.0
Electrical Energy	38	.3	44	.3
Commerce	2,362	16.6	2,837	16.6
Transportation	869	6.1	1,044	6.1
Services	4,271	30.0	5,131	30.0
Government	813	5.7	977	5.7
Unclassified	1,107	7.8	1,331	7.8
F. TAMAULIPAS				
Matamoros				
Total EAP	49,467	100.0	58,168	100.0
Primary Activities[2]	13,311	26.9	15,774	27.1
Petroleum Industry	66	.1	76	.1
Mining	131	.3	158	.3
Manufacturing	7,179	14.5	8,505	14.6
Construction	2,846	5.8	3,371	5.8
Electrical Energy	156	.3	188	.3
Commerce	6,703	13.6	7,943	13.7
Transportation	1,717	3.5	2,034	3.5
Services	12,621	25.5	14,954	25.7
Government	1,810	3.7	2,145	3.7
Unclassified	2,927	5.9	3,470	5.9
Nuevo Laredo				
Total EAP	39,463	100.0	52,928	100.0
Primary Activities[2]	4,397	11.1	5,896	11.1
Petroleum Industry	64	.2	85	.2
Mining	117	.3	159	.3
Manufacturing	7,780	19.7	10,432	19.7
Construction	2,682	6.8	3,599	6.8
Electrical Energy	146	.4	196	.4
Commerce	5,712	14.5	7,664	14.5
Transportation	1,880	4.8	2,519	4.8
Services	11,900	30.2	15,958	30.2
Government	1,779	4.5	2,387	4.5
Unclassified	3,006	7.6	4,033	7.6

Table 501 (Continued)

ECONOMICALLY ACTIVE POPULATION[1] IN MEXICAN BORDER CITIES, BY SECTOR, 1970 AND 1975

	1970		1975	
State and City	N	% of Total	N	% of Total
Reynosa				
Total EAP	38,032	100.0	42,972	100.0
Primary Activities[2]	6,122	16.1	6,914	16.1
Petroleum Industry	5,946	15.6	6,210	14.5
Mining	90	.2	99	.2
Manufacturing	4,095	10.8	4,628	10.8
Construction	2,958	7.8	3,343	7.8
Electrical Energy	144	.4	163	.4
Commerce	5,352	14.1	6,046	14.1
Transportation	1,295	3.4	1,465	3.4
Services	8,621	22.7	9,742	22.7
Government	1,243	3.3	1,405	3.3
Unclassified	2,616	6.9	2,957	6.9

1. "Economically active population" includes all persons engaged or seeking to be engaged in productive work in some branch of economic activity.
2. Includes agriculture, forestry, livestock, fisheries, and hunting.

SOURCE: Secretaría de Programación y Presupuesto, *Monografías socio-económicas de las ciudades fronterizas* (México, D.F.: Talleres Gráficos de la Nación, 1976).

Table 502

EMPLOYMENT IN U.S. BORDER COUNTIES,[1] BY SECTOR, 4 SC, 1969 AND 1976

		1969		1976	
	State	N	% of Total	N	% of Total
G.	ARIZONA				
	Total Employment	171,477	100.0	223,087	100.0
	Agricultural Services, Forestry, Fisheries	1,391	.8	1,438	.6
	Mining	7,953	4.6	8,294	3.7
	Contract Construction	11,974	7.0	11,423	5.1
	Manufacturing	10,922	6.4	16,278	7.3
	Transportation, Utilities, Communications	7,325	4.3	9,381	4.2
	Wholesale Trade	4,154	2.4	5,926	2.7
	Retail Trade	27,792	16.2	39,290	17.6
	Finance, Insurance, Real Estate	5,645	3.3	7,478	3.4
	Services	30,577	17.8	43,026	19.3
	Government	57,397	33.5	75,627	33.9
	Unclassified	6,347	3.7	4,926	2.2
H.	CALIFORNIA				
	Total Employment	278,931	100.0	846,183	100.0
	Agricultural Services, Forestry, Fisheries	6,823	.9	17,072	2.0
	Mining	2,083	.3	2,370	.3
	Contract Construction	27,646	3.8	34,097	4.1
	Manufacturing	90,880	12.5	94,297	11.1
	Transportation, Utilities, Communications	25,410	3.5	29,937	3.5
	Wholesale Trade	19,392	2.7	26,271	3.1
	Retail Trade	96,718	13.3	132,218	15.6
	Finance, Insurance, Real Estate	23,094	3.2	33,896	4.0
	Services	114,854	15.8	148,875	17.6
	Government	298,298	40.9	298,542	35.3
	Unclassified	23,733	3.3	28,608	3.4

Statistical Time Series

Table 502 (Continued)
EMPLOYMENT IN U.S. BORDER COUNTIES,[1] BY SECTOR
4 SC, 1969 AND 1976

		1969		1976	
	State	N	% of Total	N	% of Total
I.	**NEW MEXICO**				
	Total Employment	58,872	100.0	223,087	100.0
	Agricultural Services, Forestry, Fisheries	465	.8	1,438	.6
	Mining	2,547	4.6	8,294	3.7
	Contract Construction	2,723	7.0	11,423	5.1
	Manufacturing	2,942	6.4	16,278	7.3
	Transportation, Utilities, Communications	2,144	4.3	9,381	4.2
	Wholesale Trade	577	2.4	5,926	2.7
	Retail Trade	6,570	16.2	39,290	17.6
	Finance, Insurance, Real Estate	1,254	3.3	7,478	3.4
	Services	7,992	17.8	43,026	19.3
	Government	24,996	33.5	75,627	33.9
	Unclassified	2,662	3.7	4,926	2.2
J.	**TEXAS**				
	Total Employment	296,248	100.0	364,090	100.0
	Agricultural Services, Forestry, Fisheries	3,123	1.1	5,003	1.4
	Mining	3,237	1.1	4,537	1.2
	Contract Construction	13,976	4.7	15,763	4.3
	Manufacturing	34,675	11.7	52,370	14.4
	Transportation, Utilities, Communications	16,415	5.5	20,189	5.5
	Wholesale Trade	14,399	4.9	21,591	5.9
	Retail Trade	47,876	16.2	66,473	18.3
	Finance, Insurance, Real Estate	8,248	2.8	12,918	3.5
	Services	43,169	14.6	54,047	14.8
	Government	94,970	32.1	97,864	26.9
	Unclassified	16,160	5.5	13,335	3.7
	U.S. BORDER				
	Total Employment	1,251,528	100.0	1,495,642	100.0
	Agricultural Services, Forestry, Fisheries	11,802	.9	23,962	1.6
	Mining	15,820	1.3	18,156	1.2
	Contract Construction	56,319	4.5	64,558	4.3
	Manufacturing	139,419	11.1	167,088	11.2
	Transportation, Utilities, Communications	51,294	4.1	61,786	4.1
	Wholesale Trade	38,522	3.1	55,113	3.7
	Retail Trade	178,956	14.3	246,872	16.5
	Finance, Insurance, Real Estate	38,241	3.1	55,885	3.7
	Services	196,592	15.7	254,259	17.0
	Government	475,661	38.0	499,388	33.4
	Unclassified	48,902	3.9	49,205	3.3
	U.S. TOTAL				
	Total Employment	78,247,265	100.0	85,884,900	100.0
	Agricultural Services, Forestry, Fisheries	282,845	.4	376,000	.4
	Mining	622,766	.7	779,000	.9
	Contract Construction	3,617,094	4.6	3,617,000	4.2
	Manufacturing	20,270,000	25.9	19,041,000	22.2
	Transportation, Utilities, Communications	4,455,000	5.7	4,560,000	5.3
	Wholesale Trade	3,731,825	4.8	4,570,000	5.3
	Retail Trade	11,204,337	14.3	13,290,000	15.5
	Finance, Insurance, Real Estate	3,597,691	4.6	4,356,000	5.1
	Services	13,306,667	17.0	16,202,000	18.9
	Government	15,882,583	20.3	17,690,000	20.6
	Unclassified	1,276,456	1.6	1,403,900	1.6

1. Urban cores and linked counties included in economic areas defined by Bureau of Economic Analysis, U.S. Dept. of Commerce, in 1969 and covered by Southwest Regional Border Commission.

SOURCE: Niles Hansen, *The Border Economy* (Austin: University of Texas Press, 1982), pp. 170-172.

Ch. 5, Employment, Wages, and Prices   47

Table 503

HISPANIC ORIGIN WORKERS IN THE UNITED STATES: CIVILIAN LABOR FORCE, EMPLOYMENT, AND UNEMPLOYMENT, 5 SC, 1979-80

(T)

State	1979			1980		
	Civilian Labor Force	Employment	Unemployment	Civilian Labor Force	Employment	Unemployment
Arizona/Colorado/ New Mexico	403	373	30	475	423	52
California	1,649	1,508	141	1,844	1,661	181
Texas	1,057	983	74	1,120	1,024	96
U.S. Border	3,109	2,864	245	3,439	3,108	329
U.S. Total	5,019	4,684	415	5,484	4,931	554

SOURCE: U.S. Dept. of Labor, *Bureau of Labor Statistics News*, March 9, 1981.

Table 504

HISPANIC ORIGIN WORKERS IN THE UNITED STATES: UNEMPLOYMENT RATE, 5 SC, 1976-82

State	1976	1977	1978	1979	1980	1981	1982
Arizona/Colorado/ New Mexico	11.9	11.0	8.6	7.5	10.9	~	~
California	13.2	10.7	9.7	8.5	9.9	11.4	15.5
Texas	7.9	8.7	8.1	7.0	8.5	~	~
U.S. Total	11.6	10.1	8.6	8.3	10.1	~	~

SOURCE: U.S. Dept. of Labor, *Bureau of Labor Statistics News*, March 9, 1981, and *Los Angeles Times*, August 7, 1983.

Table 505

U.S. UNEMPLOYMENT RATE,[1] 4 SC, 1970-82

	State	1970	1975	1976	1977	1978	1979	1980	1981	1982[a]
G.	ARIZONA	4.1	12.1	9.8	8.2	6.1	5.1	6.7	6.1	9.2
H.	CALIFORNIA	6.0	9.9	9.2	8.2	7.1	6.2	6.8	7.4	9.4
I.	NEW MEXICO	6.3	10.0	9.1	7.8	5.8	6.6	7.5	7.3	10.1
J.	TEXAS	3.6	5.6	5.7	5.3	4.8	4.2	5.2	5.3	7.7
	U.S. Border	~	~	8.0	~	6.3	5.5	6.3	6.6	~
	U.S. Total	4.9	8.5	7.7	7.1	6.1	5.8	7.1	7.6	9.5

1. Percent unemployment of civilian population 16 years and over.
a. Through June, 1982.

SOURCE: *SAUS*, 1971-83, various tables.

Table 506
DAILY MINIMUM WAGES IN MEXICAN BORDER CITIES, 1970-81
(Pesos)

State and City	1970-71 Urban	1970-71 Rural	1972 Urban	1972 Rural	1973 Urban	1973 Rural	1974 Urban	1974 Rural	1975 Urban	1975 Rural
A. BAJA CALIF. NORTE										
Mexicali	46.00	36.00	53.85	42.50	56.65	44.70	73.10	57.70	84.90	67.00
B. CHIHUAHUA										
Ciudad Juárez	36.00	31.50	42.30	37.00	44.50	38.95	60.80	53.20	70.60	61.80
D. NUEVO LEÓN										
Monterrey	31.50	29.50	37.20	34.85	39.15	36.65	53.50	50.10	62.10	58.20
Mexico Total										
Mexico City	32.00	30.00	38.00	35.40	40.00	37.25	54.60	50.85	63.40	59.00

Table 506 (Continued)
DAILY MINIMUM WAGES IN MEXICAN BORDER CITIES, 1970-81
(Pesos)

	1976 Urban	1976 Rural	1977 Urban	1977 Rural	1978 Urban	1978 Rural	1979 Urban	1979 Rural	1980 Urban	1980 Rural	1981
A. BAJA CALIF. NORTE											
Mexicali	107.50	84.70	133.90	105.50	147.00	117.00	162.00	135.00	180.00	170.00	210.00
B. CHIHUAHUA											
Ciudad Juárez	89.40	78.20	111.30	97.30	125.00	110.00	143.00	128.00	160.00	155.00	210.00
D. NUEVO LEÓN											
Monterrey	79.90	78.80	100.40	94.10	113.00	106.00	130.00	124.00	150.00	150.00	190.00
Mexico Total											
Mexico City	84.60	78.80	106.40	79.00	120.00	113.00	138.00	131.00	163.00	163.00	210.00

SOURCE: *BM-MSD*, 1981, pp. 30-31.

Table 507

CONSUMER PRICE INDEX FOR MEXICAN BORDER CITIES, 1970-80

(1978 = 100)

State and City	1970	1971	1972	1973	1974	1975	1976	1977	1978	1979	1980[‡]
A. BAJA CALIF. NORTE Mexicali	32.2	33.9	35.9	39.3	47.9	53.8	62.1	85.3	100.0	114.7	140.0
B. CHIHUAHUA Ciudad Juárez	32.6	34.5	36.2	40.3	49.9	55.5	62.7	84.5	100.0	118.7	146.2
D. NUEVO LEÓN Monterrey	32.4	34.7	36.4	40.6	49.3	56.7	65.6	86.7	100.0	118.0	147.8
Mexico Total Mexico City	33.0	34.9	36.6	40.8	49.9	58.3	67.7	85.5	100.0	117.8	149.0

SOURCE: *BM-MSD*, 1981, p. 32.

6
Maquiladoras

Table 600

MAQUILADORA[1] CHARACTERISTICS, BY STATE AND MUNICIPALITY, 5 SC, 1970-80

(N)

Characteristic	1970	1974	1975	1976	1977	1978	1979	1980
A. BAJA CALIF. NORTE								
Ensenada								
Establishments	~	5	6	6	5	4	5	6
Employees	~	220	314	163	160	154	275	257
Average Man-Hours Worked (T)	~	~	41	26	28	24	45	41
Mexicali								
Establishments	22	57	67	69	70	65	77	79
Employees	5,002	7,888	6,324	6,604	6,351	6,543	7,965	7,146
Average Man-Hours Worked (T)	~	1	1,097	1,124	1,062	1,120	1,348	1,182
Tecate								
Establishments	~	11	10	13	11	15	20	22
Employees	~	1,098	803	717	774	640	560	672
Average Man-Hours Worked (T)	~	~	131	117	133	111	96	114
Tijuana[2]								
Establishments	16	101	99	93	92	95	101	123
Employees	2,190	9,276	7,844	7,795	7,111	8,778	10,889	12,343
Average Man-Hours Worked (T)	~	~	1,143	1,220	1,207	1,508	1,859	2,063
B. CHIHUAHUA								
Ciudad Juárez								
Establishments	22	87	86[a]	81[a]	80[a]	92[a]	103	121
Employees	3,165	18,483	19,775[a]	23,580[a]	26,792[a]	30,374[a]	36,206	39,402
Average Man-Hours Worked (T)	~	~	3,270[a]	3,968[a]	4,529[a]	5,106[a]	6,088	6,279
C. COAHUILA								
Ciudad Acuña								
Establishments	2	10	10	9	9	8	10	13
Employees	818	2,098	1,900	1,984	1,815	2,248	2,738	2,931
Average Man-Hours Worked (T)	~	~	292	332	339	398	464	476
Piedras Negras								
Establishments	5	17	12	12	12	14	16	18
Employees	1,240	2,989	2,561	2,295	2,337	2,589	2,676	2,592
Average Man-Hours Worked (T)	~	~	448	398	402	458	446	455
E. SONORA								
Agua Prieta								
Establishments	1	17	20	18	18	19	21	22
Employees	75	3,374	2,636	3,040	3,247	3,568	4,123	4,625
Average Man-Hours Worked (T)	~	~	452	529	567	626	737	782
Nogales[3]								
Establishments	5	45	38	36	37	39	47	59
Employees	1,202	9,827	6,794	7,078	7,521	8,849	12,183	12,291
Average Man-Hours Worked (T)	~	~	1,025	1,134	1,192	1,437	1,937	2,077

Table 600 (Continued)

MAQUILADORA[1] CHARACTERISTICS, BY STATE AND MUNICIPALITY, 5 SC, 1970-80
(N)

Characteristic	1970	1974	1975	1976	1977	1978	1979	1980
F. TAMAULIPAS								
Matamoros								
Establishments	23	45	40	39	37	40	46	50
Employees	2,565	9,475	9,778	10,966	11,357	11,443	15,894	15,231
Average Man-Hours Worked (T)	~	~	1,516	1,777	1,895	2,235	2,593	2,378
Nuevo Laredo								
Establishments	17	15	14	16	14	15	15	14
Employees	3,472	4,988	1,928	1,605	1,651	1,916	2,254	2,462
Average Man-Hours Worked (T)	~	~	298	248	253	293	349	384
Reynosa								
Establishments	2	12	11	9	8	9	13	17
Employees	181	1,027	1,255	1,381	1,258	2,897	4,237	5,450
Average Man-Hours Worked (T)	~	~	200	226	212	422	651	826
MEXICO BORDER								
Establishments	120	422	413	392	393	415	474	544
Employees	20,327	70,743	61,912	67,208	70,374	79,999	100,000	105,402
Average Man-Hours Worked (T)	~	~	8,770	11,099	11,819	13,738	16,613	17,057
MEXICO TOTAL								
Establishments	~	455	454	448	443	457	540	620
Employees	~	75,974	67,214	74,496	78,433	90,704	111,365	119,546
Average Man-Hours Worked (T)	~	~	10,783	12,285	13,114	15,101	18,402	19,248

1. Assembly shops.
2. Includes Rosarita, Baja California Norte.
3. Includes Magdalena de Kino, Sonora.
4. Includes Río Bravo, Tamaulipas.
a. Includes Rodrigo M. de Quevedo, Chihuahua.

SOURCE: For 1970: *LFN*, table V-8; for 1974-80: *EIME*, table 1.

Table 601

MAQUILADORA[1] CHARACTERISTICS, BY TYPE OF ECONOMIC ACTIVITY, 1974-79

(N)

Category	1974	1975	1976	1977	1978	1979
BORDER MUNICIPALITIES[2]						
Establishments	429	418	406	398	420	480
Employees	71,122	62,145	67,532	70,681	82,387	100,537
Average Man-Hours Worked	~	9,949	11,140	11,872	13,804	16,691
Food Processing						
Establishments	13	11	10	10	9	12
Employees	1,523	1,579	1,059	1,025	1,156	1,480
Average Man-Hours Worked	~	216	164	168	194	250
Shoes and Garments	111	111	114	113	112	115
Establishments	111	111	114	113	112	115
Employees	12,859	12,672	13,730	14,391	15,556	16,596
Average Man-Hours Worked	~	2,276	2,500	2,588	2,799	2,906
Furniture						
Establishments	17	10	14	16	22	31
Employees	1,367	888	1,057	1,057	1,941	2,806
Average Man-Hours Worked	~	168	192	244	344	572
Machinery (Non-Electrical)						
Establishments	22	29	30	30	27	37
Employees	2,262	2,816	2,873	2,751	3,265	4,256
Average Man-Hours Worked	~	476	492	496	570	734
Electrical Machinery						
Establishments	189	179	161	153	160	182
Employees	47,172	38,977	42,772	43,719	51,183	63,813
Average Man-Hours Worked	~	5,924	6,764	7,112	8,327	10,163
Other Manufacturing Industries						
Establishments	71	69	69	68	81	81
Employees	4,458	3,405	4,224	5,099	6,418	7,602
Average Man-Hours Worked	~	568	716	872	1,124	1,340
Service Industries						
Establishments	6	9	8	8	9	18
Employees	1,451	1,814	1,827	2,339	2,868	4,184
Average Man-Hours Worked	~	324	312	392	447	726
NON-BORDER MUNICIPALITIES						
Establishments	26	36	42	45	37	60
Employees	4,852	5,069	6,964	7,752	8,317	10,828
Average Man-Hours Worked	~	836	1,144	1,244	1,296	1,711
MEXICO TOTAL[3]						
Establishments	455	454	448	443	457	540
Employees	75,974	67,214	74,496	78,433	90,704	111,365
Average Man-Hours Worked	~	10,783	12,285	13,114	15,101	18,402

1. Assembly shops.
2. Ensenada, Mexicali, Tecate, Tijuana, Baja Calif. Norte; Ciudad Acuña, Piedras Negras, Coahuila; Ciudad Juárez, Chihuahua; Agua Prieta, Nogales, Sonora; Matamoros, Nuevo Laredo, Reynosa, Tamaulipas.
3. Totals may not add up due to rounding.

SOURCE: *EIME,* table 7.

Ch. 6, Maquiladoras 55

Table 602

PERSONNEL EMPLOYED IN MAQUILADORA[1] INDUSTRY, BY STATE AND MUNICIPALITY, 5 SC, 1974-80

(N)

State and Municipality	1974	1975	1976	1977	1978	1979	1980
A. BAJA CALIF. NORTE							
Ensenada							
Total Personnel	220	314	163	160	154	275	257
Workers	~	297	153	150	141	255	235
Men	~	97	69	85	39	48	50
Women	~	200	84	65	102	207	185
Production Technicians	~	6	5	5	5	9	10
Supervisors	~	11	5	5	8	11	12
Mexicali							
Total Personnel	7,888	6,324	6,604	6,351	6,543	7,465	7,146
Workers	~	5,551	5,683	5,648	5,773	6,978	6,183
Men	~	1,272	1,241	1,203	1,443	1,646	1,546
Women	~	4,279	4,622	4,445	4,330	5,332	4,637
Production Technicians	~	516	509	481	539	685	674
Supervisors	~	257	232	222	231	302	289
Tecate							
Total Personnel	1,098	803	717	774	640	560	672
Workers	~	738	644	697	591	508	599
Men	~	108	112	122	226	215	251
Women	~	603	532	575	365	293	348
Production Technicians	~	31	47	52	30	28	42
Supervisors	~	34	26	25	19	24	31
Tijuana[2]							
Total Personnel	9,276	7,844	7,795	7,111	8,778	10,889	12,343
Workers	~	6,722	6,730	6,309	7,760	9,738	10,841
Men	~	1,406	1,498	1,617	1,829	2,196	2,414
Women	~	5,316	5,232	4,692	5,931	7,542	8,427
Production Technicians	~	692	584	352	552	637	876
Supervisors	~	430	481	450	466	514	626
B. CHIHUAHUA							
Ciudad Juárez							
Total Personnel	18,483	19,775	23,580	26,792	30,374	36,206	39,402
Workers	~	17,303	20,662	23,558	26,712	31,140	33,648
Men	~	3,640	4,214	4,914	5,661	6,250	6,868
Women	~	13,663	16,448	18,644	21,051	24,890	26,780
Production Technicians	~	1,370	1,589	1,856	2,117	3,021	3,408
Supervisors	~	1,102	1,329	1,378	1,545	2,045	2,346
C. COAHUILA							
Ciudad Acuña							
Total Personnel	2,098	1,900	1,984	1,815	2,248	2,738	2,931
Workers	~	1,558	1,617	1,590	2,018	2,403	2,570
Men	~	307	291	266	358	385	441
Women	~	1,251	1,326	1,324	1,660	2,018	2,129
Production Technicians	~	263	285	152	115	211	243
Supervisors	~	79	82	73	115	124	118
Piedras Negras							
Total Personnel	2,989	2,561[3]	2,295[3]	2,337[3]	2,589[3]	2,676	2,592
Workers	~	2,288	2,045	2,065	2,303	2,389	2,311
Men	~	188	362	402	561	580	536
Women	~	2,100	1,683	1,663	1,742	1,809	1,775
Production Technicians	~	197	177	191	222	213	192
Supervisors	~	76	73	81	64	74	89
E. SONORA							
Agua Prieta							
Total Personnel	3,374	2,636	3,090	3,247	3,568	4,123	4,625
Workers	~	2,177	2,621	2,765	3,068	3,528	3,919

Table 602 (Continued)

PERSONNEL EMPLOYED IN MAQUILADORA[1] INDUSTRY, BY STATE AND MUNICIPALITY, 5 SC, 1974-80

(N)

State and Municipality	1974	1975	1976	1977	1978	1979	1980
Men	~	631	706	706	856	940	1,171
Women	~	1,546	1,915	2,059	2,212	2,588	2,748
Production Technicians	~	369	377	388	408	482	574
Supervisors	~	90	92	94	92	113	132
Nogales[4]							
Total Personnel	9,827	6,794	7,078	7,521	8,849	12,183	12,921
Workers	~	5,633	6,021	6.260	7,287	10,174	10,785
Men	~	2,180	2,258	2,453	3.037	3,932	4,357
Women	~	3,453	3,763	3,807	4,250	6,242	6,428
Production Technicians	~	738	696	836	1,104	1,413	1,458
Supervisors	~	423	361	425	458	596	678
F. TAMAULIPAS							
Matamoros							
Total Personnel	9,475	9,778	10,966	11,357	13,443	15,894	15,231
Workers	~	8,528	9,519	9,793	11,645	13,841	13,053
Men	~	1,432	1,528	1,791	2,219	2,611	2,314
Women	~	7,096	7,992	8,002	9,426	11,230	10,739
Production Technicians	~	765	1,018	1,112	1,222	1,352	1,469
Supervisors	~	485	428	452	576	701	709
Nuevo Laredo							
Total Personnel	4,988	1,928	1,605	1,651	1,916	2,254	2,462
Workers	~	1,691	1,458	1,488	1,684	1,985	2,205
Men	~	250	221	225	324	472	430
Women	~	1,441	1,237	1,263	1,360	1,513	1,775
Production Technicians	~	168	92	104	173	203	184
Supervisors	~	69	55	59	59	66	73
Reynosa[5]							
Total Personnel	1,027	1,255	1,381	1,258	2,897	4,237	5,450
Workers	~	1,083	1,229	1,136	2,353	3,523	4,529
Men	~	91	108	92	402	889	937
Women	~	992	1,121	1,044	1,951	2,634	3,592
Production Technicians	~	81	83	72	241	264	413
Supervisors	~	91	69	50	303	450	508
Mexico Border							
Total Personnel	70,743	61,912	67,258	70,374	81,999	100,000	106,032
Workers	~	53,569	58,562	61,684	71,335	86,462	90,878
Men	~	12,232	13,140	13,876	16,955	20,614	21,315
Women	~	41,337	45,422	47,808	54,380	66,298	69,563
Production Technicians	~	5,196	5,462	5,601	6,728	8,518	9,543
Supervisors	~	3,147	3,234	3,089	3,936	5,020	5,611
Mexico Total							
Total Personnel	75,974	67,214	74,496	78,433	90,704	111,365	119,546
Workers	~	57,850	64,670	68,187	78,570	95,818	102,020
Men	~	12,575	13,686	14,999	18,205	21,981	23,140
Women	~	45,275	50,984	53,188	60,365	73,837	78,880
Production Technicians	~	5,924	6,165	6,348	7,543	9,569	10,828
Supervisors	~	3,440	3,661	3,898	4,591	5,978	6,698

1. Assembly shops.
2. Includes Rosarito, Baja California Norte.
3. Includes Rodrigo M. Quevedo, Chihuahua.
4. Includes Magdalena de Kino, Sonora.
5. Includes Río Bravo, Tamaulipas.

SOURCE: *EIME*, table 2.

Table 603

PERSONNEL EMPLOYED IN MAQUILADORA[1] INDUSTRY, BY TYPE OF ECONOMIC ACTIVITY, 1974-79

(N)

Category	1974	1975	1976	1977	1978	1979
Border Municipalities[2]						
Total Personnel	71,122	62,145	67,542	70,681	82,387	100,537
Workers	~	53,771	58,806	61,738	71,669	86,879
Men	~	11,653	12,656	13,957	17,074	20,343
Women	~	42,118	46,150	47,771	54,595	66,536
Production Technicians	~	5,216	5,483	5,624	6,762	8,613
Supervisors	~	3,158	3,243	3,329	3,956	5,045
Food Processing						
Total Personnel	1,523	1,579	1,059	1,025	1,156	1,480
Workers	~	1,505	1,009	966	1,074	1,368
Men	~	364	257	164	215	271
Women	~	1,141	752	802	859	1,097
Production Technicians	~	26	13	25	34	43
Supervisors	~	48	37	34	48	69
Shoes and Garments						
Total Personnel	12,889	12,672	13,730	14,391	15,556	16,596
Workers	~	11,652	12,577	13,146	14,168	15,010
Men	~	2,096	2,272	2,646	2,751	2,831
Women	~	9,556	10,305	10,500	11,417	12,179
Production Technicians	~	670	768	836	966	1,096
Supervisors	~	350	385	409	422	490
Furniture						
Total Personnel	1,367	888	1,057	1,357	1,941	2,806
Workers	~	816	981	1,261	1,785	2,481
Men	~	754	952	1,217	1,718	2,217
Women	~	62	29	44	67	264
Production Technicians	~	15	19	23	60	165
Supervisors	~	57	57	73	96	160
Machinery (Non-electrical)						
Total Personnel	2,262	2,810	2,863	2,751	3,265	4,256
Workers	~	2,365	2,359	2,313	2,744	3,540
Men	~	1,801	1,787	1,682	2,015	2,221
Women	~	564	572	631	729	1,319
Production Technicians	~	295	364	324	419	556
Supervisors	~	150	140	114	102	160
Electrical Machinery						
Total Personnel	47,172	38,977	42,772	43,719	51,183	63,613
Workers	~	32,757	36,430	37,383	43,577	53,844
Men	~	5,108	5,655	6,306	7,973	9,795
Women	~	27,649	30,775	31,077	35,604	44,049
Production Technicians	~	3,920	3,982	3,964	4,711	6,088
Supervisors	~	2,300	2,360	2,372	2,895	3,681
Other Manufacturing Industries						
Total Personnel	4,458	3,405	4,224	5,099	6,418	7,602
Workers	~	3,004	3,787	4,516	5,709	6,828
Men	~	1,379	1,617	1,838	2,275	2,726
Women	~	1,625	2,170	2.678	3,434	4,102
Production Technicians	~	228	267	370	459	502
Supervisors	~	173	170	213	250	272
Service Industries						
Total Personnel	1,451	1,814	1,827	2,339	2,868	4,184
Workers	~	1,672	1,663	2,143	2,612	3,808
Men	~	151	116	104	127	282
Women	~	1,521	1,547	3,039	3,485	3,526
Production Technicians	~	62	70	82	113	163
Supervisors	~	80	94	114	143	213

Table 603 (Continued)

PERSONNEL EMPLOYED IN MAQUILADORA[1] INDUSTRY, BY TYPE OF ECONOMIC ACTIVITY, 1974-79

(N)

Category	1974	1975	1976	1977	1978	1979
Non-Border Municipalities						
Total Personnel	4,852	5,069	6,964	7,752	8,317	10,828
Workers	~	4,079	5,864	6,459	6,901	8,939
Men	~	922	1,030	1,042	1,131	1,638
Women	~	3,157	4,834	5,417	5,770	7,301
Production Technicians	~	708	682	724	781	956
Supervisors	~	282	418	569	635	933
Mexico Total[3]						
Total Personnel	75,974	67,214	74,496	78,433	90,704	111,365
Workers	~	57,850	64,670	68,187	78,570	95,818
Men	~	12,575	13,686	14,999	18,205	21,981
Women	~	45,275	50,984	53,188	60,365	73,837
Production Technicians	~	5,924	6,165	6,348	7,543	9,569
Supervisors	~	3,440	3,661	3,898	4,591	5,978

1. Assembly shops.
2. Ensenada, Mexicali, Tecate, Tijuana, Baja California Norte; Ciudad Acuña, Piedras Negras, Coahuila; Ciudad Juárez, Chihuahua; Agua Prieta, Nogales, Sonora; Matamoros, Nuevo Laredo, Reynosa, Tamaulipas.
3. Totals may not add up due to rounding.

SOURCE: *EIME*, table 8.

7
Transportation and Communication

Table 700
LENGTH OF ROADS,[1] 10 SC, 1960–80

PART I. T km

	State	1960	1965	1970	1971	1972	1973	1974	1975	1976	1977	1978	1979	1980
A.	BAJA CALIF. NORTE	1.2	1.3	1.5	1.5	1.9	2.4	2.7	2.8	3.0	3.3	3.4	3.4	3.5
B.	CHIHUAHUA	1.9	2.4	3.0	3.3	6.0	8.0	8.4	8.9	8.9	9.2	9.5	9.6	9.7
C.	COAHUILA	2.5	2.6	2.9	3.0	6.2	7.5	8.2	8.5	9.1	9.3	9.6	9.6	9.7
D.	NUEVO LEÓN	1.8	2.3	2.5	2.6	3.8	4.3	4.6	4.9	5.4	4.7	5.9	5.9	5.9
E.	SONORA	2.7	3.0	3.6	4.6	8.1	8.5	9.5	9.8	10.5	10.8	11.1	11.5	11.6
F.	TAMAULIPAS	2.0	2.3	2.6	3.0	7.5	8.1	8.4	9.1	9.8	10.0	10.3	10.5	10.6
	Mexico Border	12.1	13.9	16.1	18.0	33.5	38.8	41.8	44.0	46.7	47.3	49.8	50.5	51.0
	Mexico Total	45.1	58.3	71.8	77.5	122.6	154.5	175.4	186.2	193.3	199.1	207.7	211.2	212.6
G.	ARIZONA	59.7	62.9	68.7	75.6	79.3	82.7	83.8	83.0	89.8	88.5	92.5	97.7	121.0
H.	CALIFORNIA	237.1	264.3	264.1	267.2	268.0	272.9	272.9	275.3	278.1	282.0	283.7	286.1	290.8
I.	NEW MEXICO	105.4	106.9	108.3	110.1	109.6	113.1	113.0	113.6	114.1	113.6	115.9	115.9	121.3
J.	TEXAS	371.4	387.0	395.1	399.6	403.1	404.8	408.5	411.8	414.7	415.9	421.8	426.3	430.5
	U.S. Border	773.6	821.1	836.2	852.5	860.0	873.6	878.2	883.9	896.7	899.9	913.9	926.0	963.7
	U.S. Total	5,706.1	5,938.0	6,003.0	6,049.4	6,094.1	6,126.6	6,140.9	6,176.8	6,207.9	6,224.0	6,253.1	6,305.1	6,430.0

PART II. T Miles

	State	1960	1965	1970	1971	1972	1973	1974	1975	1976	1977	1978	1979	1980
A.	BAJA CALIF. NORTE	.7	.8	.9	.9	1.2	1.5	1.7	1.7	1.9	2.0	2.1	2.1	2.2
B.	CHIHUAHUA	1.2	1.5	1.9	2.0	3.7	5.0	5.2	5.5	5.5	5.7	5.9	6.0	6.0
C.	COAHUILA	1.6	1.6	1.8	1.9	3.9	4.7	5.1	5.3	5.7	5.8	6.0	6.0	6.0
D.	NUEVO LEÓN	1.1	1.4	1.6	1.6	2.4	2.7	2.9	3.0	3.4	2.9	3.7	3.7	3.7
E.	SONORA	1.7	1.9	2.2	2.9	5.0	5.3	5.9	6.1	6.5	6.7	6.9	7.1	7.2
F.	TAMAULIPAS	1.2	1.4	1.6	1.9	4.7	5.0	5.2	5.7	6.1	6.2	6.4	6.5	6.6
	Mexico Border	7.5	8.6	10.0	11.2	20.8	24.1	26.0	27.3	29.0	29.4	30.9	31.4	31.7
	Mexico Total	28.0	36.2	44.6	48.2	76.2	96.0	109.0	115.7	120.1	123.7	129.1	131.2	132.1
G.	ARIZONA	37.1	39.1	42.7	47.0	49.3	51.4	52.1	51.6	55.8	55.0	57.5	60.7	75.2
H.	CALIFORNIA	147.3	164.2	164.1	166.0	166.5	169.6	169.6	171.1	172.8	175.2	176.3	177.8	180.7
I.	NEW MEXICO	65.5	66.4	67.3	68.4	68.1	70.3	70.2	70.6	70.9	70.6	72.0	72.0	75.4
J.	TEXAS	230.8	240.5	245.5	248.3	250.5	251.5	253.8	255.9	257.7	258.4	262.1	264.9	267.5
	U.S. Border	480.7	510.2	519.6	529.7	534.4	542.8	545.7	549.2	557.2	559.2	567.9	575.4	598.8
	U.S. Total	3,545.6	3,689.7	3,730.1	3,758.9	3,786.7	3,806.9	3,815.8	3,838.1	3,857.4	3,867.4	3,885.5	3,917.8	3,995.4

1. U.S. data exclude federal highways.

SOURCE: Mexico: *AEM*, 1960–81, various tables.
United States: U.S. Bureau of Public Roads, *Highway Statistics*, 1961–70;

Table 701

MOTOR VEHICLES REGISTERED, 10 SC, 1960-80

(T)

	State and Category	1960	1965	1970	1971	1972	1973	1974	1975	1976	1977	1978	1979	1980
A.	BAJA CALIF. NORTE													
	Autos, Buses, Trucks	39.1	63.6	70.3	84.0	85.8	144.1	156.3	188.0	194.1	220.7	322.6	359.0	380.7
	Motorcycles	.3	3.8	1.4	1.8	1.9	1.5	2.0	2.1	2.2	3.0	3.5	2.6	2.7
B.	CHIHUAHUA													
	Autos, Buses, Trucks	29.4	30.6	25.7	36.4	34.8	123.0	132.2	173.3	193.6	186.8	202.8	139.2	141.0
	Motorcycles	.3	1.6	3.9	5.3	5.6	6.4	7.5	11.3	12.4	12.7	13.7	15.3	15.1
C.	COAHUILA													
	Autos, Buses, Trucks	16.9	20.1	31.6	34.6	38.4	68.0	80.7	105.6	108.1	111.3	120.4	231.4	256.7
	Motorcycles	.5	1.3	3.9	7.1	5.1	6.2	8.9	9.4	7.1	6.2	6.0	8.9	4.7
D.	NUEVO LEÓN													
	Autos, Buses, Trucks	27.2	45.7	63.9	71.1	81.7	118.6	138.8	163.0	177.2	188.1	197.2	227.3	261.9
	Motorcycles	.7	2.7	7.2	8.2	6.1	8.3	8.9	9.5	7.2	8.5	8.5	12.9	13.9
E.	SONORA													
	Autos, Buses, Trucks	19.0	32.4	38.3	33.5	43.4	90.3	84.9	102.1	112.2	144.5	165.6	174.9	176.2
	Motorcycles	.2	1.9	6.9	4.1	3.7	4.8	6.2	5.7	5.5	8.1	8.3	8.7	8.8
F.	TAMAULIPAS													
	Autos, Buses, Trucks	15.5	19.4	24.2	25.2	37.7	112.7	129.1	142.5	147.7	156.9	193.9	213.6	230.0
	Motorcycles	.1	.8	1.6	3.2	2.2	2.5	2.8	3.1	3.2	3.9	3.9	4.5	4.9
	Mexico Border													
	Autos, Buses, Trucks	147.1	211.8	254.0	284.8	321.8	656.7	722.0	874.5	932.9	1,008.3	1,202.5	1,345.4	1,446.5
	Motorcycles	2.1	12.1	24.9	29.7	24.6	29.7	36.3	41.1	37.6	42.4	43.9	52.9	50.1
	Mexico Total													
	Autos, Buses, Trucks	483.1	771.1	1,233.8	1,342.2	1,520.1	2,398.8	2,823.2	3,339.6	3,621.1	3,947.9	4,712.2	5,222.4	5,827.8
	Motorcycles	24.4	54.2	136.9	159.9	168.3	185.8	216.8	246.5	222.5	283.2	309.4	342.0	341.9
G.	ARIZONA													
	Autos, Buses, Trucks	624	825	1,093	1,185	1,302	1,419	1,524	1,522	1,491	1,554	1,665	1,769	1,866
	Motorcycles	8.6	14.4	34.3	42.9	43	57	65	73	71	65	63	72	82

Table 701 (Continued)
MOTOR VEHICLES REGISTERED, 10 SC, 1960–80
(T)

State and Category	1960	1965	1970	1971	1972	1973	1974	1975	1976	1977	1978	1979	1980
H. CALIFORNIA													
Autos, Buses, Trucks	7,799	9,989	11,901	12,324	12,852	13,413	13,787	14,034	14,102	14,958	15,577	16,261	16,801
Motorcycles	79.6	268.2	567.8	614.6	615	646	671	699	674	679	683	662	754
I. NEW MEXICO													
Autos, Buses, Trucks	426	525	637	661	711	726	751	791	863	907	989	1,031	1,061
Motorcycles	7.4	9.3	21.8	27.4	27	31	33	36	37	39	42	46	49
J. TEXAS													
Autos, Buses, Trucks	4,457	5,610	6,693	6,984	7,316	7,816	8,203	8,299	8,674	9,489	10,152	10,001	10,219
Motorcycles	47.0	60.4	144.6	186.2	186	245	268	309	286	286	290	218	307
U.S. Border													
Autos, Buses, Trucks	13,306	16,949	20,324	21,154	22,181	23,374	24,265	24,646	25,130	26,908	28,383	29,067	29,947
Motorcycles	142.6	352.3	768.5	871.1	871	979	1,037	1,117	1,068	1,069	1,078	998	1,192
U.S. Total													
Autos, Buses, Trucks	73,858	90,358	108,418	112,922	118,618	125,157	130,751	133,727	137,287	142,381	148,778	154,118	159,029
Motorcycles	575.5	1,380.7	2,814.7	3,343.9	3,345	4,378	4,969	5,494	5,110	5,015	5,138	4,984	5,823

SOURCE: Mexico: *AEM*, 1960–81, various tables.
United States: *SAUS*, 1960–81, various tables.

Table 702
AIRPORTS, 10 SC, 1964-81
(N)

	State	1964	1970	1971	1972	1973	1974	1975	1976	1977	1978	1979	1980	1981
A.	BAJA CALIF. NORTE	25	?	?	?	?	53	?	55	55	56	56	57	57
B.	CHIHUAHUA	74	?	?	?	?	89	?	103	108	91	93	103	108
C.	COAHUILA	36	?	?	?	?	14	?	17	17	19	19	33	19
D.	NUEVO LEÓN	16	?	?	?	?	40	?	40	41	41	40	38	40
E.	SONORA	53	?	?	?	?	48	?	50	51	48	51	60	57
F.	TAMAULIPAS	38	?	?	?	?	36	?	36	36	35	35	40	39
	Mexico Border	242	?	?	?	?	280	?	301	308	290	294	331	320
	Mexico Total	1,043	?	?	?	?	1,113	1,186	1,189	1,262	1,199	1,208	1,312	1,320
G.	ARIZONA	185	215	209	198	196	196	196	202	209	209	210	216	224
H.	CALIFORNIA	627	730	746	754	753	769	781	804	813	822	819	825	832
I.	NEW MEXICO	114	127	129	131	134	134	134	139	139	142	145	149	156
J.	TEXAS	812	982	1,128	1,167	1,169	1,192	1,213	1,217	1,250	1,298	1,332	1,375	1,431
	U.S. Border	1,738	2,054	2,212	2,250	2,252	2,291	2,324	2,362	2,411	2,471	2,506	2,565	2,643
	U.S. Total	9,490	11,261	12,070	12,405	12,700	13,062	13,251	13,770	14,069	14,574	14,746	15,115	15,422

SOURCE: Mexico: *AEM*, 1965-81.
United States: FAA, *Statistical Handbook of Aviation*, 1965-81.

Table 703

TELEPHONES IN USE, 10 SC, 1960-81

(T)

	State	1960	1965	1970	1971	1972	1973	1974	1975	1976	1977	1978	1979	1980	1981
A.	BAJA CALIF. NORTE	?	22.2	34.3	36.6	40.7	43.5	46.2	46.5	49.9	51.7	47.0	50.8	56.2	66.4
B.	CHIHUAHUA	?	24.2	37.1	40.9	47.1	55.5	70.2	87.6	104.3	119.8	134.1	149.8	166.6	180.7
C.	COAHUILA	?	26.8	38.1	40.2	47.4	53.9	44.4	73.3	86.7	97.1	105.6	118.2	149.0	87.7
D.	NUEVO LEÓN	?	44.7	94.0	106.8	122.1	140.2	157.3	178.2	206.6	228.0	253.2	277.4	300.7	323.1
E.	SONORA	?	18.0	33.9	36.3	42.2	55.5	66.3	77.2	88.4	98.0	112.2	126.2	165.9	152.0
F.	TAMAULIPAS	?	25.4	43.0	48.7	56.1	64.2	74.2	84.9	107.6	126.6	138.1	147.5	165.9	208.5
	Mexico Border		161.3	280.4	309.5	355.6	412.8	458.6	547.7	643.5	721.2	790.2	869.9	1,004.3	1,018.4
	Mexico Total	532.0	827.7	1,516.7	1,724.0	1,967.9	2,236.1	2,542.2	2,928.3	3,325.2	3,736.8	4,157.8	4,552.8	5,024.2	5,536.6
G.	ARIZONA	439	645	956	1,055	1,166	1,279	1,372	1,444	1,517	1,630	1,796	1,970	2,109	?
H.	CALIFORNIA	6,365	10,596	13,306	13,751	14,381	15,100	15,755	16,454	17,178	18,104	19,123	20,164	20,881	?
I.	NEW MEXICO	280	394	494	531	569	608	637	674	711	756	813	861	878	?
J.	TEXAS	3,146	4,556	6,329	6,680	7,122	7,541	8,001	8,447	8,970	9,573	10,245	10,803	11,344	?
	U.S. Border	10,230	16,191	21,085	22,017	23,238	24,528	25,765	27,019	28,376	30,063	31,977	33,798	35,212	?
	U.S. Total	64,980	93,659	120,155	125,141	131,602	138,288	143,970	149,008	155,173	162,072	169,027	175,535	180,424	182,000†

SOURCE: Mexico: *AEM*, 1960-81.
United States: U.S. Federal Communications Commission, *Statistics of Communications Common Carriers*, 1961-82.

Table 704

FILMS SHOWN IN MEXICO, BY NATIONAL ORIGIN,[1] 6 SC, 1966-80

(N)

State and Category	1966	1967	1968	1969	1970	1971	1972	1973	1974	1975	1976	1977	1978	1979	1980
A. BAJA CALIF. NORTE															
Total	8,103	8,323	7,997	7,830	7,386	6,794	6,620	6,937	6,892	6,808	6,597	6,690	5,829	5,447	4,894
Mexican	4,001	3,847	3,732	3,857	3,911	3,393	3,099	3,449	3,562	3,581	3,219	2,953	2,235	2,382	2,065
American	3,399	3,607	3,287	2,837	2,413	2,271	2,073	1,767	1,570	1,378	1,555	1,823	2,135	2,156	1,942
Italian	178	206	240	311	310	348	486	660	580	643	631	775	756	337	354
B. CHIHUAHUA															
Total	23,839	25,654	26,077	25,752	26,067	24,907	23,809	27,718	21,782	20,717	18,297	17,834	17,653	16,259	15,987
Mexican	11,157	12,744	12,884	13,243	13,619	13,215	13,404	13,036	12,369	11,923	10,283	9,481	9,009	8,224	7,833
American	10,153	10,426	10,145	9,727	9,506	8,934	8,606	7,765	5,946	5,168	4,740	5,470	6,169	5,350	5,862
Italian	616	625	597	654	740	729	630	845	1,037	1,204	1,038	1,229	996	1,144	1,042
C. COAHUILA															
Total	25,785	31,501	30,035	27,662	27,375	28,674	27,502	26,062	23,306	20,883	18,843	16,467	14,389	14,639	14,547
Mexican	12,531	16,325	15,489	14,949	14,641	15,728	14,773	13,936	12,168	11,061	9,732	7,973	7,027	7,547	7,680
American	11,620	13,335	12,713	11,017	11,077	11,067	10,924	10,237	8,818	7,433	6,932	6,551	5,455	5,359	5,330
Italian	444	434	535	395	431	568	527	568	775	791	885	783	877	900	894
D. NUEVO LEÓN															
Total	38,876	40,229	38,151	36,090	32,617	31,799	29,865	25,438	23,776	22,305	18,676	15,954	15,690	14,358	14,481
Mexican	22,791	24,451	23,578	23,555	21,672	20,850	19,643	16,118	14,926	14,521	11,981	9,804	9,180	8,739	9,047
American	10,153	13,652	12,743	10,728	9,112	9,388	8,857	7,996	7,143	6,172	5,119	4,747	5,176	4,281	4,202
Italian	616	500	415	370	520	517	388	427	469	562	651	546	615	653	677
E. SONORA															
Total	28,632	27,820	27,131	25,738	23,221	21,200	19,151	18,904	19,493	18,410	17,111	16,258	14,574	11,547	9,514
Mexican	15,414	14,253	14,015	13,464	11,548	11,715	11,190	9,873	9,792	9,366	8,314	7,859	6,390	5,166	4,369
American	10,019	10,321	10,087	9,581	8,869	7,600	5,733	5,913	5,822	4,956	5,158	5,151	5,354	4,225	3,697
Italian	927	840	680	746	757	690	652	926	1,424	1,677	1,501	1,423	1,414	1,081	778
F. TAMAULIPAS															
Total	40,260	38,635	38,692	35,394	32,823	32,765	31,939	28,728	25,847	24,466	21,649	18,833	16,474	15,487	14,539
Mexican	23,578	22,428	22,102	20,714	19,212	20,509	19,595	16,894	14,523	13,454	11,664	10,146	8,958	8,318	7,690
American	14,326	14,431	14,892	13,091	11,734	10,997	10,998	10,436	9,654	9,185	8,119	7,118	6,114	5,826	5,338
Italian	523	448	491	413	436	357	431	444	482	526	654	714	629	208	173
Mexico Border															
Total	165,495	172,162	171,086	158,466	149,489	146,139	138,886	133,787	121,096	113,589	101,173	93,036	84,609	77,737	73,962
Mexican	89,472	94,048	91,800	89,782	84,603	84,810	81,704	73,306	67,340	63,906	55,193	48,216	42,799	40,376	38,684
American	59,670	65,772	63,867	56,981	52,711	51,257	47,191	44,114	38,953	34,292	31,623	30,860	34,283	27,197	26,371
Italian	3,304	3,053	2,958	2,889	3,194	3,209	3,114	3,870	3,767	5,403	5,360	5,470	5,287	4,323	3,918
Mexico Total															
Total	548,559	589,548	582,329	560,725	538,349	523,551	505,661	487,991	469,568	457,570	431,205	417,858	405,170	378,008	358,039
Mexican	292,534	322,213	321,060	315,823	310,739	306,739	300,253	286,186	269,887	263,062	245,806	233,922	223,951	205,382	193,380
American	212,666	220,729	214,521	200,608	184,122	175,617	164,961	156,813	146,698	136,258	129,759	130,904	129,501	123,851	121,880
Italian	11,892	13,386	12,528	11,348	10,568	10,666	10,580	13,212	15,803	17,807	18,324	19,266	21,092	20,051	17,961

1. As of 1980, countries following Italy with next largest shares of Mexican film market included Japan, France, England, and Spain, in that order (based on Mexico Total).

SOURCE: *AEM*, 1967–81, various tables.

8

Agricultural and Fisheries Production

Table 800
CORN PRODUCTION, 8 SC, 1975-80

PART I. Area = T Ha.; Production = T MET

	State	1975 Area	1975 Production	1976 Area	1976 Production	1977 Area	1977 Production	1978 Area	1978 Production	1979 Area	1979 Production	1980 Area	1980 Production
A.	BAJA CALIF. NORTE	7	13	4	17	2	6	4	12	9	19	?	?
B.	CHIHUAHUA	221	192	271	193	231	192	131	152	217	161	?	?
C.	COAHUILA	24	36	81	66	42	58	48	69	27	56	?	?
D.	NUEVO LEÓN	26	26	95	98	90	103	62	79	52	68	?	?
E.	SONORA	21	81	10	27	20	58	18	53	27	104	?	?
F.	TAMAULIPAS	217	430	273	457	483	869	297	603	222	569	?	?
	Mexico Border	516	778	734	858	868	1,286	560	968	554	977	?	?
	Mexico Total	6,694	8,449	6,783	8,017	7,470	10,174	7,191	10,930	5,581	8,457	?	?
H.	CALIFORNIA	103	707	117	807	100	732	114	883	105	757	109	908
J.	TEXAS	445	2,851	628	4,693	668	3,760	583	3,634	510	3,331	526	2,952
	U.S. Border	548	3,558	745	5,500	768	4,492	697	4,517	615	4,088	635	3,860
	U.S. Total	27,087	145,521	28,866	158,113	28,343	160,409	29,121	183,396	29,312	200,238	29,798	167,752

PART II. Area = T Acres; Production = T Bushels

	State	1975 Area	1975 Production	1976 Area	1976 Production	1977 Area	1977 Production	1978 Area	1978 Production	1979 Area	1979 Production	1980 Area	1980 Production
A.	BAJA CALIF. NORTE	17	515	10	674	5	238	10	476	22	753	?	?
B.	CHIHUAHUA	546	3,646	669	7,649	571	7,609	324	6,024	536	6,380	?	?
C.	COAHUILA	59	1,427	200	2,616	104	2,299	119	2,734	67	2,219	?	?
D.	NUEVO LEÓN	64	1,030	234	3,884	222	4,082	153	3,131	128	2,695	?	?
E.	SONORA	52	3,210	25	1,070	49	2,299	44	2,100	67	4,122	?	?
F.	TAMAULIPAS	536	17,041	674	18,111	1,193	34,438	734	23,897	548	22,549	?	?
	Mexico Border	1,275	30,832	1,813	34,003	2,144	50,964	1,383	38,362	1,368	38,719	?	?
	Mexico Total	16,534	334,834	16,754	317,714	18,450	403,195	17,762	433,156	13,785	335,151	?	?
H.	CALIFORNIA	254	28,000	290	32,000	247	29,000	281	35,000	260	30,000	270	36,000
J.	TEXAS	1,100	113,000	1,550	186,000	1,650	149,000	1,440	144,000	1,260	132,000	1,300	117,000
	U.S. Border	1,354	141,000	1,840	218,000	1,897	178,000	1,681	179,000	1,520	162,000	1,570	153,000
	U.S. Total	66,905	5,767,000	71,300	6,266,000	70,006	6,357,000	71,930	7,268,000	72,400	7,939,000	73,061	6,648,000

SOURCE: Mexico: *AEM*, 1976–81.
United States: *USDA-CP*, 1976–81.

Table 801
COTTON PRODUCTION, 9 SC, 1975-80

PART I. Area = T. Ha.; Production = T MET

	State	1975 Area	1975 Production	1976 Area	1976 Production	1977 Area	1977 Production	1978 Area	1978 Production	1979 Area	1979 Production	1980 Area	1980 Production
A.	BAJA CALIF. NORTE	35	28	34	31	53	48	50	59	57	59	?	?
B.	CHIHUAHUA	15	8	19	16	33	29	28	26	39	30	?	?
C.	COAHUILA	40	41	38	46	49	51	44	51	45	41	?	?
E.	SONORA	41	39	43	47	107	126	86	99	99	110	?	?
F.	TAMAULIPAS	#	#	4	2	10	5	3	1	3	1	?	?
	Mexico Border	131	116	138	142	252	259	211	236	243	241	?	?
	Mexico Total	227	206	235	224	420	416	350	366	375	349	?	?
G.	ARIZONA	121	133	150	193	226	247	232	244	250	293	255	311
H.	CALIFORNIA	354	426	453	541	563	608	589	423	250	742	607	677
I.	NEW MEXICO	40	16	29	17	55	38	50	25	57	24	51	25
J.	TEXAS	1,588	522	1,825	722	2,621	1,198	2,521	832	2,766	1,497	2,783	729
	U.S. Border	2,103	1,096	2,457	1,472	3,464	2,091	3,391	1,524	3,735	2,267	3,697	1,742
	U.S. Total	3,561	1,809	4,419	2,364	5,376	3,233	5,020	2,365	5,195	3,187	5,350	2,423

PART II. Area = T Acres; Production = T Net Bales

	State	1975 Area	1975 Production	1976 Area	1976 Production	1977 Area	1977 Production	1978 Area	1978 Production	1979 Area	1979 Production	1980 Area	1980 Production
A.	BAJA CALIF. NORTE	86	129	84	142	131	220	124	270	141	271	?	?
B.	CHIHUAHUA	37	37	47	73	82	133	69	119	96	138	?	?
C.	COAHUILA	99	188	94	211	121	234	109	234	111	505	?	?
E.	SONORA	101	179	106	216	264	578	212	454	245	505	?	?
F.	TAMAULIPAS	#	#	10	9	25	23	7	5	7	5	?	?
	Mexico Border	323	533	341	652	622	1,189	521	1,083	600	1,106	?	?
	Mexico Total	561	946	580	1,028	1,037	1,909	865	1,680	926	1,602	?	?
G.	ARIZONA	298	611	370	884	557	1,135	572	1,122	618	1,347	631	1,426
H.	CALIFORNIA	875	1,954	1,120	2,482	1,390	2,790	1,455	1,940	1,635	3,408	1,500	3,109
I.	NEW MEXICO	98	73	71	76	137	173	123	114	141	112	127	114
J.	TEXAS	3,923	2,394	4,508	3,315	6,473	5,500	6,228	3,819	6,831	5,539	6,873	3,345
	U.S. Border	5,194	5,032	6,069	6,757	8,557	9,598	8,378	6,995	9,225	10,406	9,131	7,994
	U.S. Total	8,796	8,302	10,914	10,581	13,279	14,389	12,400	10,856	12,831	14,629	13,215	11,122

SOURCE: Mexico: *AEM*, 1976–81.
United States: *USDA-CP*, 1976–81.

Table 802
WHEAT PRODUCTION, 10 SC, 1975–80

PART I. Area = T. Ha.; Production = T MET

	State	1975 Area	1975 Production	1976 Area	1976 Production	1977 Area	1977 Production	1978 Area	1978 Production	1979 Area	1979 Production	1980 Area	1980 Production
A.	BAJA CALIF. NORTE	38	134	56	243	72	315	63	218	71	211	?	?
B.	CHIHUAHUA	85	250	84	258	65	257	37	121	52	215	?	?
C.	COAHUILA	33	59	26	50	27	58	21	95	15	31	?	?
D.	NUEVO LEÓN	16	23	14	24	10	16	14	31	20	48	?	?
E.	SONORA	299	1,346	374	1,783	248	1,013	285	1,156	166	806	?	?
F.	TAMAULIPAS	1	2	1	1	#	1	#	1	1	2	?	?
	Mexico Border	472	1,814	555	2,359	422	1,660	420	1,622	325	1,313	?	?
	Mexico Total	778	2,798	894	3,363	709	3,456	760	2,785	584	2,287	?	?
G.	ARIZONA	105	495	174	879	57	275	56	264	51	259	87	468
H.	CALIFORNIA	405	1,693	381	1,625	274	1,189	269	1,162	324	1,538	466	2,327
I.	NEW MEXICO	178	310	106	185	172	248	136	163	166	245	202	286
J.	TEXAS	2,308	3,568	1,903	2,814	1,903	3,198	1,093	1,470	1,862	3,756	2,105	3,538
	U.S. Border	2,996	6,067	2,564	5,504	2,406	4,910	1,554	3,059	2,403	5,797	2,860	6,619
	U.S. Total	28,211	58,078	28,652	58,302	26,808	55,144	22,872	48,340	25,285	58,083	28,685	64,507

PART II. Area = T Acres; Production = T Bushels

	State	1975 Area	1975 Production	1976 Area	1976 Production	1977 Area	1977 Production	1978 Area	1978 Production	1979 Area	1979 Production	1980 Area	1980 Production
A.	BAJA CALIF. NORTE	94	4,923	138	8,928	178	11,573	156	8,009	175	7,752	?	?
B.	CHIHUAHUA	210	7,185	207	9,479	161	9,442	91	4,446	128	7,899	?	?
C.	COAHUILA	82	2,168	64	1,837	67	2,131	52	3,490	37	1,139	?	?
D.	NUEVO LEÓN	40	845	35	882	25	588	35	1,139	540	1,764	?	?
E.	SONORA	739	49,452	924	65,507	613	37,218	704	42,471	410	29,612	?	?
F.	TAMAULIPAS	2	73	2	37	#	37	#	37	2	73	?	?
	Mexico Border	1,166	66,646	1,371	86,670	1,042	60,988	1,037	59,592	1,292	48,239	?	?
	Mexico Total	1,922	102,799	2,208	123,556	1,751	126,973	1,877	102,321	1,442	84,024	?	?
G.	ARIZONA	260	18,200	431	32,300	140	10,100	138	9,700	125	9,500	215	17,200
H.	CALIFORNIA	1,001	62,200	940	59,700	678	43,700	665	42,700	800	56,500	1,150	85,500
I.	NEW MEXICO	440	11,400	262	6,800	425	9,100	336	6,000	410	9,000	500	10,500
J.	TEXAS	5,700	131,100	4,700	103,400	4,700	117,500	2,700	54,000	4,600	138,000	5,200	130,000
	U.S. Border	7,401	222,900	6,333	202,200	5,943	180,400	3,839	112,400	5,935	213,000	7,065	243,200
	U.S. Total	69,656	2,133,800	70,771	2,142,000	66,216	2,026,000	56,495	1,776,000	62,454	2,134,000	70,853	3,370,000

SOURCE: Mexico: *AEM*, 1976–81.
United States: *USDA-CP*, 1976–81.

Table 803

FISHERIES PRODUCTION,[1] 7 SC, 1960-80

PART I. T MET

State	1960	1965	1970	1971	1972	1973	1974	1975	1976	1977	1978	1979	1980
A. BAJA CALIF. NORTE	44.0	64.1	61.3	59.7	63.6	59.6	80.1	130.5	163.0	229.3	233.3	279.0	340.1
B. CHIHUAHUA	#	.2	.2	.2	.2	.5	.1	~	#	.2	.2	.3	.3
C. COAHUILA	.1	.1	.1	.1	.1	.1	.1	#	#	.1	.3	.4	1.1
E. SONORA	9.6	12.0	37.4	60.0	69.4	74.3	56.9	90.3	98.5	84.3	126.1	135.2	252.9
F. TAMAULIPAS	9.0	5.6	8.5	9.2	10.3	13.6	14.4	15.2	14.6	18.7	25.0	27.7	27.8
Mexico Border	62.7	82.0	107.5	129.2	143.6	148.1	151.6	236.0	276.1	332.6	384.9	442.6	622.2
Mexico Total	142.4	199.8	273.5	302.1	313.2	343.7	348.9	451.3	524.7	562.1	703.5	850.5	1,058.6
H. CALIFORNIA	245.4	207.7	318.9	264.4	294.4	331.6	310.7	396.9	416.0	396.4	327.5	330.2	364.7
J. TEXAS	117.0	69.9	66.7	75.8	52.2	44.5	42.6	39.0	42.2	49.0	44.9	36.3	42.6
U.S. Border	362.4	277.6	385.6	340.2	346.6	376.0	353.3	435.9	458.1	445.4	372.4	366.5	407.3
U.S. Total	2,242.1	2,167.3	2,230.4	2,276.7	2,179.5	2,203.1	2,249.9	2,211.8	2,426.8	2,465.3	2,734.3	2,842.7	2,934.8

PART II. M Pounds

State	1960	1965	1970	1971	1972	1973	1974	1975	1976	1977	1978	1979	1980
A. BAJA CALIF. NORTE	97	141	135	132	159	149	201	327	409	575	514	615	750
B. CHIHUAHUA	#	#	#	#	#	1	#	~	#	#	#	1	1
C. COAHUILA	#	#	#	#	#	#	#	#	#	#	1	1	2
E. SONORA	21	26	82	132	174	186	143	226	247	211	316	339	634
F. TAMAULIPAS	20	12	19	20	26	34	36	38	37	47	63	69	70
Mexico Border	138	181	237	285	360	371	380	592	692	834	965	1,109	1,560
Mexico Total	314	440	603	757	785	862	875	1,131	1,315	1,409	1,763	2,132	2,654
H. CALIFORNIA	541	458	703	583	649	731	685	875	917	874	722	728	804
J. TEXAS	258	154	147	167	115	98	94	86	93	108	99	80	94
U.S. Border	799	612	850	750	764	829	779	961	1,010	982	821	808	898
U.S. Total	4,943	4,778	4,917	5,019	4,805	4,857	4,960	4,876	5,350	5,435	6,028	6,267	6,470

1. Weight of catch.

SOURCE: Mexico: *AEM* 1960-81.
United States: U.S. National Oceanic and Atmospheric Administration, *Fishery Statistics of the U.S.*, 1961-81.

9
Mexican–U.S. Economic Relations

Table 900

PESO-DOLLAR EXCHANGE RATE,[1] 1930-82

(U per US)

Year		Year	
1930	2.006	1957	12.491
1931	2.467	1958	12.491
1932	3.492	1959	12.491
1933	3.464	1960	12.491
1934	3.605	1961	12.491
1935	3.560	1962	12.491
1936	3.602	1963	12.491
1937	3.604	1964	12.491
1938	4.520	1965	12.491
1939	5.181	1966	12.491
1940	5.392	1967	12.491
1941	4.869	1968	12.491
1942	4.862	1969	12.491
1943	4.860	1970	12.491
1944	4.859	1971	12.491
1945	4.859	1972	12.500
1946	4.859	1973	12.500
1947	4.860	1974	12.500
1948	5.302	1975	12.500
1949	7.924	1976	14.459
1950	8.643	1977	22.604
1951	8.648	1978	22.781
1952	8.630	1979	22.816
1953	8.615	1980	22.968
1954	11.047	1981	24.547
1955	12.491	1982	72.990
1956	12.491		

1. 12-month average.
SOURCE: *Federal Reserve Bulletin*, 1930-82.

Table 901

PESO-DOLLAR EXCHANGE RATE, JANUARY-DECEMBER, 1982

(U per US)

Month		Month	
January	26.469	July	48.594
February	31.736	August	90.187
March	45.366	September	101.86
April	46.152	October	108.83
May	46.903	November	130.61
June	47.716	December	147.35

SOURCE: *Federal Reserve Bulletin*, various issues, 1982 and 1983.

Table 902

MEXICAN–U.S. TRADE TOTALS, 1900-80

(M US)

	U.S. Imports from Mexico			U.S. Exports to Mexico		
Year	Amount (M US)	% of U.S. Imports from Western Hemisphere	% of Total U.S. Imports	Amount (M US)	% of U.S. Exports to Western Hemisphere	% of Total U.S. Exports
1900	29	12.9	3.4	35	15.4	2.5
1901	29	11.4	3.5	36	14.9	2.4
1902	40	14.8	4.4	40	16.5	2.9
1903	41	13.8	4.0	42	16.4	3.0
1904	44	13.8	4.4	46	16.1	3.1
1905	46	12.2	4.1	46	14.5	3.0
1906	51	13.6	4.2	58	15.1	3.3
1907	57	13.4	4.0	66	15.3	3.5
1908	47	12.9	3.9	56	13.7	3.0
1909	48	11.5	3.7	50	12.9	3.0
1910	59	11.7	3.8	58	12.1	3.3
1911	57	11.7	3.7	61	10.8	3.0
1912	66	12.0	4.0	53	8.2	2.4
1913	78	13.4	4.3	54	7.1	2.2
1914	93	14.3	4.9	39	6.0	1.6
1915	78	10.6	4.7	34	5.9	1.2
1916	105	9.7	4.4	54	4.7	1.0
1917	130	8.8	4.4	111	7.1	1.8
1918	159	10.0	5.2	98	6.0	1.6
1919	149	8.1	3.8	131	7.5	1.7
1920	179	7.4	3.4	208	8.1	2.5
1921	119	11.3	4.7	222	15.8	4.9
1922	132	11.2	4.2	110	9.6	2.9
1923	140	9.5	3.7	120	8.9	2.9
1924	167	11.4	4.6	135	9.6	2.9
1925	179	11.9	4.2	145	9.4	3.0
1926	169	10.7	3.8	135	8.3	2.8
1927	138	9.2	3.3	109	6.4	2.2
1928	125	8.2	3.1	116	6.4	2.3
1929	118	7.3	2.7	134	6.9	2.6
1930	80	6.7	2.6	116	8.5	3.0
1931	48	5.8	2.3	52	6.9	2.1
1932	37	6.9	2.8	32	6.9	2.0
1933	31	6.0	2.1	38	8.4	2.3
1934	36	5.7	2.2	55	8.5	2.6
1935	42	5.4	2.1	66	9.3	2.9
1936	49	5.4	2.0	76	9.3	3.1
1937	60	5.4	1.9	109	9.4	3.3
1938	49	6.5	2.5	62	6.0	2.0
1939	56	6.2	2.4	83	7.3	2.6
1940	76	7.0	2.9	97	6.5	2.4
1941	98	5.9	2.9	159	7.8	3.1
1942	124	7.0	4.5	148	6.7	1.8
1943	192	7.8	5.7	187	7.7	1.4
1944	204	6.9	5.2	264	10.0	1.9
1945	231	8.0	5.6	307	12.0	3.1
1946	232	8.4	4.7	505	13.7	5.2
1947	247	7.3	4.3	630	10.2	4.4
1948	246	6.0	3.5	522	9.8	4.1
1949	243	6.1	3.7	468	9.6	3.9

Table 902 (Continued)

MEXICAN–U.S. TRADE TOTALS, 1900-80
(M US)

	U.S. Imports from Mexico			U.S. Exports to Mexico		
Year	Amount (M US)	% of U.S. Imports from Western Hemisphere	% of Total U.S. Imports	Amount (M US)	% of U.S. Exports to Western Hemisphere	% of Total U.S. Exports
1950	315	6.2	3.6	526	10.7	5.1
1951	326	5.6	3.0	730	11.0	4.9
1952	410	6.8	3.8	683	10.2	4.5
1953	355	5.8	3.3	663	10.2	4.2
1954	328	5.6	3.2	649	10.0	4.3
1955	397	6.3	3.5	719	10.4	4.6
1956	401	5.8	3.2	860	10.4	4.5
1957	430	6.1	3.3	917	10.2	4.4
1958	454	6.8	3.5	904	11.3	5.0
1959	435	6.2	2.9	755	9.8	4.3
1960	443	6.5	3.0	831	10.8	4.0
1961	538	7.7	3.7	828	10.8	3.9
1962	578	7.6	3.5	821	10.6	3.8
1963	594	7.6	3.5	873	11.0	3.7
1964	643	7.7	3.4	1,107	12.0	4.2
1965	638	6.9	3.0	1,104	11.1	4.0
1966	750	6.9	3.0	1,180	10.3	3.9
1967	749	6.4	2.8	1,222	10.3	3.9
1968	910	6.4	2.7	1,378	10.3	4.0
1969	1,029	6.6	2.9	1,450	9.9	3.8
1970	1,219	7.2	3.1[a]	1,704	10.9	3.9[a]
1971	1,262	6.7	2.8[a]	1,620	9.6	3.7[a]
1972	1,632	7.4	2.9[a]	1,982	10.1	4.0[a]
1973	2,306	8.4	3.3[a]	2,937	11.7	4.1[a]
1974	3,386	8.3	3.4[a]	4,855	13.6	4.9[a]
1975	3,066	8.0	3.2[a]	5,141	13.2	4.8[a]
1976	3,598	8.3	3.0[a]	4,990	12.1	4.3[a]
1977	4,694	9.3	3.2[a]	4,822	11.0	4.0[a]
1978	6,094	10.8	3.5[a]	6,680	13.3	4.6[a]
1979	8,800	12.8	4.3[a]	9,847	16.0	5.4[a]
1980	12,519	16.0	5.2[a]	15,145	20.4	6.9[a]

a. Includes estimates for low-valued shipments from countries which could not be identified because of illegible reporting on import entries.

SOURCE: *HSUS*, 1975, vol. II, series U335-352 and U317-334; *SAUS*, 1971-1980, various series.

Table 903

U.S. GOVERNMENT GRANTS AND CREDITS TO MEXICO, 1945-80

(M US)

Year	Amount (M US)	% of Western Hemisphere	% of Total U.S. Foreign Grants and Credits
1945	2	.20	.10
1946	35	41.66	.61
1947	58	52.25	.95
1948	20	34.48	.36
1949	33	45.21	.58
1950	19	29.69	.45
1951	−5[a]	- -	- -
1952	29	31.87	.51
1953	18	4.80	.28
1954	27	39.71	.53
1955	−10[a]	- -	- -
1956	−8[a]	- -	- -
1957	23	9.09	.45
1958	78	13.73	1.58
1959	14	4.14	.36
1960	21	10.82	.46
1961	83	11.67	1.96
1962	3	.51	.07
1963	−18	- -	- -
1964	−55	- -	- -
1965	38	5.90	.75
1966	54	7.31	.98
1967	50	7.63	.75
1968	53	6.58	.78
1969	16	2.64	.24
1970	−1[a]	- -	- -
1971	−18[a]	- -	- -
1972	−10[a]	- -	- -
1973	−4[a]	- -	- -
1974	95	11.51	1.30
1975	70	8.56	.81
1976	34	6.56	.43
1977	75	17.32	1.11
1978	17	5.80	.21
1979	103	28.53	1.33
1980	80	11.68	.74

a. Minus figures (−) occur when the total of grant returns, principal repayments, and/or foreign currencies disbursed by the U.S. government exceeds new grants and new credits utilized and/or acquisitions of foreign currencies through new sales of farm products.

SOURCE: *HSUS*, 1975, vol. II, series U75-186; and *SAUS*, 1971-1980, various series.

10
Tourism

Table 1000
BORDER TOURISTS, BY STATE AND PORT OF ENTRY, 5 SC, 1971-79
(N)

State	1971	1972	1973	1974	1975	1976	1977	1978	1979
A. BAJA CALIF. NORTE									
Mexicali									
Total Entering	87,726	87,330	92,783	89,383	71,345	57,104	58,569	50,389	53,169
Residents Abroad									
Mexicans	24,781	24,642	27,082	25,696	19,520	16,571	16,928	12,019	11,504
Foreigners	62,945	62,688	65,701	63,687	51,825	40,533	41,641	38,370	41,665
Total Departing	506	210	128	129	136	186	93	129	574
Tijuana									
Total Entering	74,916	79,215	84,578	95,091	96,585	92,501	86,136	78,488	79,164
Residents Abroad									
Mexicans	23,520	25,229	25,816	23,656	20,159	15,157	11,851	8,249	7,521
Foreigners	51,396	53,986	58,762	71,435	76,426	77,344	74,285	70,239	71,643
Total Departing	1,260	1,530	1,438	1,840	2,366	1,736	845	384	582
State Total									
Total Entering	44,766	44,238	44,112	265,582	234,640	202,934	193,977	184,629	183,965
Residents Abroad									
Mexicans	340	314	303	49,976	40,959	32,947	30,223	21,477	20,553
Foreigners	44,426	43,924	43,809	215,606	193,681	169,987	163,754	163,152	163,412
Total Departing	281	288	228	1,980	2,514	1,939	956	1,409	1,262
B. CHIHUAHUA									
Ciudad Juárez									
Total Entering	155,010	165,905	177,743	176,118	186,104	185,139	194,700	189,823	194,738
Residents Abroad									
Mexicans	44,045	44,772	48,387	50,707	58,156	62,718	69,547	64,137	68,083
Foreigners	110,965	121,133	129,406	125,411	127,948	122,421	125,153	125,686	126,655
Total Departing	7,182	5,826	5,884	1,655	877	723	548	658	3,587
State Total									
Total Entering	86,408	90,543	101,409	222,954	236,977	234,382	245,552	242,724	251,188
Residents Abroad									
Mexicans	25,489	26,126	26,486	59,827	69,557	75,625	84,513	80,195	86,387
Foreigners	60,919	64,417	74,923	163,127	167,420	158,757	161,039	162,529	164,791
Total Departing	2,596	2,455	2,338	3,300	2,297	2,443	2,544	2,073	5,667

Table 1000 (Continued)

BORDER TOURISTS, BY STATE AND PORT OF ENTRY, 5 SC, 1971–79
(N)

State	1971	1972	1973	1974	1975	1976	1977	1978	1979
C. COAHUILA									
Piedras Negras									
Total Entering	85,943	113,700	97,513	95,886	103,224	103,636	100,127	80,150	78,200
Residents Abroad									
Mexicans	34,384	44,974	44,274	42,994	47,847	51,159	48,659	31,800	33,032
Foreigners	51,559	68,726	53,239	52,892	55,377	52,477	51,468	48,350	45,168
Total Departing	625	439	229	176	236	158	109	246	5,591
State Total									
Total Entering	94,130	127,701	150,577	126,837	135,320	135,051	135,390	111,593	108,554
Residents Abroad									
Mexicans	36,253	54,044	47,862	54,684	60,127	62,208	62,793	46,000	47,432
Foreigners	58,057	76,560	102,715	72,153	75,193	72,843	72,597	65,593	61,122
Total Departing	1,079	686	663	414	578	2,964	353	545	6,883
E. SONORA									
Nogales									
Total Entering	201,351	222,046	244,916	210,361	198,099	168,954	158,120	181,058	194,297
Residents Abroad									
Mexicans	18,072	22,962	26,087	26,870	31,571	33,768	36,339	41,465	42,536
Foreigners	183,279	199,084	218,899	183,491	166,528	134,826	121,781	139,593	151,761
Total Departing	584	219	917	291	1,161	593	810	715	2,638
San Luis Río Colorado									
Total Entering	26,170	25,348	27,959	21,610	16,636	12,994	11,825	11,743	13,540
Residents Abroad									
Mexicans	8,097	9,521	10,901	8,980	6,996	5,785	5,308	5,573	6,294
Foreigners	18,073	15,827	17,058	12,630	9,640	7,209	6,517	6,170	7,246
Total Departing	~	7	7	3	2	9	60	9	157
State Total									
Total Entering	283,284	298,672	293,182	447,702	422,669	366,672	330,929	384,726	416,045
Residents Abroad									
Mexicans	18,565	22,989	23,865	52,070	55,064	57,336	58,398	67,740	76,141
Foreigners	264,719	275,683	269,317	395,632	367,605	309,336	272,531	316,986	339,904
Total Departing	281	392	322	2,887	4,830	4,147	2,922	2,984	5,583

Table 1000 (Continued)
BORDER TOURISTS, BY STATE AND PORT OF ENTRY, 5 SC, 1971–79
(N)

State	1971	1972	1973	1974	1975	1976	1977	1978	1979
F. TAMAULIPAS									
Ciudad Reynosa									
Total Entering	118,809	137,457	143,840	153,077	158,456	152,033	162,829	168,058	173,978
Residents Abroad									
Mexicans	13,683	16,381	19,081	19,035	24,316	30,161	35,897	38,674	42,147
Foreigners	105,126	121,076	124,759	134,042	134,140	121,872	126,932	129,384	131,841
Total Departing	1,299	956	933	912	798	781	711	1,115	4,352
Matamoros									
Total Entering	72,050	79,736	84,433	95,998	96,507	89,026	86,321	89,600	86,915
Residents Abroad									
Mexicans	5,001	5,944	7,514	9,468	10,381	11,653	11,593	12,801	13,584
Foreigners	67,049	73,792	76,919	86,530	86,126	77,373	74,728	76,799	73,331
Total Departing	6,004	7,138	7,635	9,333	8,681	9,088	7,931	7,056	7,403
Nuevo Laredo									
Total Entering	326,377	360,943	370,482	357,299	353,256	318,265	313,846	318,508	317,931
Residents Abroad									
Mexicans	30,992	34,943	38,780	41,907	46,857	50,972	55,993	63,452	67,635
Foreigners	295,385	326,050	331,702	315,392	306,399	267,293	257,853	255,056	250,296
Total Departing	2,248	2,341	2,199	1,551	2,041	1,740	1,406	1,162	10,201
State Total									
Total Entering	42,454	48,575	47,596	673,209	679,053	628,820	632,928	647,869	651,479
Residents Abroad									
Mexicans	3,604	4,121	4,862	86,316	100,060	112,973	123,649	137,001	145,612
Foreigners	38,850	44,454	42,734	586,893	578,993	515,847	509,279	510,868	505,867
Total Departing	3,023	3,060	2,298	12,995	12,561	12,801	11,346	10,621	25,633
Mexico Border									
Total Entering	551,222	609,732	636,876	1,736,284	1,708,659	1,567,859	1,538,776	1,571,541	1,611,231
Residents Abroad									
Mexicans	84,251	107,694	103,378	248,189	325,767	341,089	359,576	352,413	376,125
Foreigners	466,971	505,038	533,498	1,488,095	1,382,892	1,226,770	1,179,200	1,219,128	1,235,095
Total Departing	7,260	6,881	5,849	21,576	24,586	24,294	18,121	17,632	45,028

Table 1000 (Continued)
BORDER TOURISTS, BY STATE AND PORT OF ENTRY, 5 SC, 1971–79
(N)

State	1971	1972	1973	1974	1975	1976	1977	1978	1979
Mexico Total									
Total Entering	2,769,987	3,214,497	3,579,739	3,761,884	3,735,202	3,656,483	3,721,066	4,371,873	4,897,675
Residents Abroad									
Mexicans	271,340	308,045	337,571	344,653	372,232	397,893	430,305	456,560	515,303
Foreigners	2,238,593	2,604,189	2,901,183	3,006,800	2,844,431	2,691,656	2,830,479	3,300,802	3,622,172
Total Departing	2,266,012	2,657,829	2,966,352	3,089,943	3,044,904	2,994,351	3,079,982	3,670,319	4,111,985

SOURCE: *AEM*, 1972–81, various tables.

Table 1001
TOURISM AND BORDER TRANSACTIONS: MEXICAN REVENUE AND EXPENDITURES, 1970–80
(M US)

	1970	1971	1972	1973	1974	1975	1976	1977	1978	1979	1980[‡]
Revenue	1,465.1	1,637.1	1,875.3	2,250.5	2,491.8	2,724.8	3,102.1	2,942.4	3,484.7	4,362.5	5,330.7
Tourism	415.0	461.0	562.6	724.2	842.0	800.1	835.6	866.5	1,121.0	1,443.3	1,670.1
Border Transactions	1,050.1	1,176.1	1,312.7	1,526.3	1,649.8	1,924.7	2,266.5	2,075.9	2,363.7	2,919.2	3,660.6
Expenditure	1,019.6	1,068.9	1,198.7	1,406.7	1,644.2	2,034.6	2,270.0	1,757.0	2,150.8	2,954.8	4,067.2
Tourism	191.4	201.0	259.7	303.0	391.6	445.8	423.1	396.0	519.0	713.6	1,010.8
Border Transactions	828.2	867.9	939.0	1,103.7	1,252.6	1,588.8	1,846.9	1,361.0	1,631.8	2,241.2	3,056.4
Balance	445.5	568.2	676.6	843.8	847.6	690.2	832.1	1,185.4	1,333.9	1,407.7	1,263.5

SOURCE: *BM-MSD*, 1981, p. 32.

Table 1002

U.S. TOURISTS IN MEXICO, BY U.S. STATE OF DEPARTURE, 4 SC, 1932-73

		1932	1933	1934	1935	1936	1937	1938	1939	1940	1942	1943
G.	ARIZONA	2,620	2,391	3,755	3,636	4,019	5,192	5,448	6,120	5,787	5,541	7,680
H.	CALIFORNIA	4,779	5,042	8,583	9,577	12,290	16,156	13,497	17,302	18,864	10,254	14,440
I.	NEW MEXICO	516	424	730	759	1,056	1,269	1,351	1,467	1,531	1,073	2,072
J.	TEXAS	28,070	30,225	40,964	40,601	45,226	56,890	48,902	66,721	47,361	51,950	79,640
	U.S. Border Total	35,985	38,082	54,032	54,573	62,591	79,867	69,198	97,730	73,543	68,818	103,832
	U.S. Total	45,462	48,442	73,756	85,055	107,228	144,955	119,616	147,666	139,626	99,752	132,573

		1944	1945	1946	1947	1948	1949	1950	1951	1952	1953	1954
G.	ARIZONA	6,768	8,182	10,674	14,717	19,908	23,324	31,487	31,930	30,201	28,008	30,602
H.	CALIFORNIA	15,819	20,999	33,270	31,984	34,072	39,294	63,867	66,427	70,703	70,605	88,168
I.	NEW MEXICO	2,286	2,059	3,066	2,904	3,944	6,083	8,039	8,657	9,249	8,453	9,338
J.	TEXAS	66,290	86,017	116,896	103,440	106,456	132,249	150,911	143,225	164,493	161,966	183,542
	U.S. Border Total	91,163	117,257	163,906	153,045	164,380	200,950	254,304	250,239	274,646	98,613	311,650
	U.S. Total	125,369	165,988	267,005	253,758	265,853	316,252	391,126	412,815	442,568	424,070	495,969

		1955	1956	1957	1958	1959	1960	1961	1962	1963	1964	1965
G.	ARIZONA	28,389	34,583	36,747	41,565	49,226	50,727	57,842	77,473	100,177	118,708	134,340
H.	CALIFORNIA	95,280	109,990	125,668	126,831	140,963	151,332	170,967	221,108	263,205	301,813	319,112
I.	NEW MEXICO	9,879	9,663	9,901	11,093	12,296	11,371	11,694	12,400	13,603	16,046	18,513
J.	TEXAS	183,502	197,601	197,476	208,943	221,763	219,576	228,270	284,695	309,608	372,429	410,408
	U.S. Border Total	317,050	351,837	369,792	388,432	424,248	433,006	468,773	595,676	686,593	808,996	882,373
	U.S. Total	532,834	593,281	625,104	657,567	712,615	719,138	760,202	897,534	1,012,959	1,159,811	1,266,260

		1966	1967	1968	1969	1970	1971	1972	1973
G.	ARIZONA	132,442	153,166	178,874	193,594	220,890	243,538	255,158	249,539
H.	CALIFORNIA	394,162	395,185	418,777	454,699	492,981	545,505	602,969	614,999
I.	NEW MEXICO	17,674	22,078	23,835	27,021	30,941	32,545	33,865	42,242
J.	TEXAS	413,271	494,538	508,244	568,606	592,480	648,536	740,091	740,505
	U.S. Border Total	957,549	1,064,967	1,129,730	1,243,920	1,337,292	1,470,124	1,632,083	1,647,285
	U.S. Total	1,414,453	1,560,707	1,665,978	1,846,686	1,980,873	2,209,804	2,535,060	2,758,113

SOURCE: *AEM*, 1939-78, various tables.

Part Two
Development of Data

11

The Economy of Baja California

Mike Farrell

One of the most rapidly developing areas of the world, the State of Baja California, Mexico, is of considerable interest to academicians and practitioners in the field of economic and social development. With the growth of the state's economy has come an expansion of interrelationships with the United States. The international character of this interchange invests it with a special significance as it presents unique problems as well as opportunities for ordinary citizens to enter directly into the world of foreign affairs. This study summarizes the economic situation and the development plans and programs under way in Baja California. The hope is that greater understanding of the problems of a developing region will enable the United States and Mexico to become better neighbors for the benefit of citizens on both sides of the frontier.

Evolution of the Economy

The population data shown in table 1100 attest to the region's rapid growth. The total population has grown at a rate of 7.2% (compounded continuously) during the forty years prior to the 1970 census, while urban growth has averaged almost 8.4% annually. As a result, the population of Baja California is highly urbanized (85.5% in 1970) and is concentrated in the border cities of Mexicali and Tijuana. The *municipios* (municipalities) of the same names contain 88% of the population and an even greater proportion of economic activity.

Data on the economy of the area are sparse. There are no official time series on production or expenditure, and the occasional censuses of industry have concentrated on the gross value of production. Mexico's Central Bank, however, has compiled input-output (I-O) data for 1965. A private firm elaborated on these data in a study performed for the state government in 1970, thus providing a basic source of information for the years 1965 and 1969. Rather than relying directly on the estimated values of state output, it seems more prudent to first employ the proportional shares of output to investigate the structure of the economy.

Kuznets was able to show a broad relationship between the structure of an economy and the level of per capita income.[1] For comparison, the value added estimates from the I-O tables for 1965 and 1969 have been organized in accordance with Kuznets's presentation of the

---

[1] Simon Kuznets, *The Economic Growth of Nations* (Cambridge, Mass.: Harvard University Press, 1971).

Table 1100

BAJA CALIFORNIA RURAL AND URBAN POPULATION, 1930-70

Year	Total	Rural	Urban
1930	48,327	22,059	26,268
1940	79,907	39,030	39,877
1950	226,965	80,574	146,391
1960	520,165	116,102	404,063
1970	870,421	125,684	744,737

SOURCE: *Compendio de estadísticas básicas, Estado de Baja California, México* (Tijuana, B.C.: Instituto de Investigaciones Económicas y Sociales, Universidad Autónoma de Baja California, 1975), table 7, p. 39 (hereafter referred to as *Compendio*).

production structure in fifty-seven countries. The results appear in table 1101.

A comparison of the data in table 1101 with Kuznets's original estimates (table 1102) reveals that Baja California's production structure most closely resembles that of country groups VI and VII, which had a mean 1958 per capita GDP of $540 and $864, respectively. The I-O tables indicate that Baja California's per capita GDP was $890 in 1965 and $851 in 1969. In view of Kuznets's findings, the structure of the Baja California economy seems to be broadly consistent with these figures.

The main peculiarity of the state's production structure relative to Kuznets's groups VI and VII is that the services sector accounts for 10% to 15% more of GDP and the manufacturing sector is correspondingly less important. Also, the rapid decline in the relative importance of agriculture in just four years (table 1101) is not due to the rapid growth of other activities, as one might expect in the course of economic development, since it reflects a sharp fall in the production of cotton, the principal crop, owing to infestation of the pink bollworm and the increased salinity of the Colorado River in the Mexicali Valley.[2] If, rather than falling by an estimated 222.9 million pesos, the value of cotton output had merely remained at the 1965 level, agriculture's relative share would have exceeded 11% in 1969.

Before commenting further on the services sector, it is interesting to compare Kuznets's results with labor force

---

[2] Both of these afflictions came from the United States. The bollworm infestation spread to Mexico via Arizona and the salinization of the river resulting from the construction of drainage canals designed to relieve the salt buildup in the Walton-Mohawk irrigation district.

Table 1101

BAJA CALIFORNIA SHARE OF PRODUCTION IN GDP, 1965 AND 1969[a]

Share of Production	1965	1969
Agriculture	12.3	8.9
Industry	35.3	38.8
Mining	1.7	1.7
Manufacturing	20.8	23.5
Construction	4.4	4.6
Electricity	1.3	1.5
Transport and Communications	7.1	7.5
Services	52.5	52.1
Trade	12.9	12.6
Banks, Insurance, and Real Estate	1.9	1.8
Dwellings	9.3	9.6
Other (including hotels, restaurants, and amusements)	28.1 (12.5)	28.1 (12.5)

a. The original data represent value added at market prices. Value added at factor cost was obtained by the subtraction of commercial margins on the basis of Martínez's estimates that the trade sector accounted for 965.9 and 1,106.3 million pesos in 1965 and 1969 (*Posibilidades*, p. 67). Shares of the other sectors were reduced in proportion to their contribution to GDP with the exception of "Dwellings" which was treated as representing factor cost since it is largely an imputed figure.

SOURCE: *El Estado de Baja California y sus posibilidades de desarrollo*, Bufete de Estudios Económicos del Sr. Lic. Gustavo Martínez Cabanas, Tijuana, B.C., 1971, table 9, p. 22, and table 17, pp. 315-316 (hereafter referred to as *Posibilidades*).

shares and relative product per worker in the various sectors of the Baja California economy. Tables 1103 and 1104 present these comparisons. Baja California bears a closer resemblance to the group V countries with a mean per capita GDP of $382 (table 1103), indicating that in a sense Baja California's employment structure is not as highly developed as the GDP level would imply. The relative productivity comparison (available from Kuznets only for "benchmark" values of per capita GDP) reflects the "less advanced" pattern of employment in Baja California, indicating that the economy is most similar to the $500 per capita pattern (table 1104). Most striking is the extremely low relative productivity of labor in agriculture, implying a larger than normal gap between the degree of modernization of Baja California agriculture and the rest of the economy.

Factors Affecting Service Sector Shares

A major problem for developing nations is the provision of employment opportunities for the rapidly growing labor force. It has become commonplace to regard the services sector as a sort of dumping ground where the otherwise openly unemployed join the ranks of the disguised unemployed as redundant retail clerks, domestics, shoeshine boys, and the like. Some have even gone so far as to regard the excess of the rate of growth of service employment over that of manufacturing jobs as a proxy measure of the excess supply of labor.[3] Baja California is typical of developing economies in that underemployment is viewed as the major economic problem. Reliable information on the extent of excess labor does not exist. The Secretary of Industry and Commerce estimated Baja California's underemployment as ranging between 12.3% and 16.6% for the late 1960s.[4] Open unemployment at the time of the 1970 census was estimated to be 16,945 persons, or 7.6% of the economically active population.[5]

Another possible indicator of employment problems is the labor force participation (LFP) rate. Baja California reports an LFP of 25.5%. At first glance, this appears to be extremely low, but it is largely attributable to the young age of the population resulting from the high natural rate of growth. Forty-seven percent of Baja California's population was fourteen years or younger in 1970, only slightly more than the 46.2% of the total Mexican population in this age group. Baja California's LFP is below that of Mexico, estimated at 26.9% in 1970. Interestingly, Baja California's female LFP (18.1%) exceeds the female Mexican average of 16.4% indicating that it is the male labor force which accounts for the differences between Baja California and all Mexico. Table 6 details the male and female LFP by age for Mexico, Baja California, and the municipalities of Tijuana and Mexicali.

The lower participation rate of the school-age groups reflects the higher rate of school attendance in Baja California relative to Mexico as a whole. With 1.8% of the total population, Baja California registered 2% of primary school students and 2.8% secondary school students in Mexico in 1972.[6] The lower male LFP rates may reflect a "discouraged worker" effect, but they may also stem in part from the far superior standard of living and the small importance of agriculture in Baja California compared with the rest of the country. The latter may be borne out by the generally higher LFP for older men in Mexicali relative to Tijuana, the former municipality being much more dependent on agriculture for employment and also having a lower per capita income.

---

[3]Alan T. Udall, "The Effects of Rapid Increases in Labor Supply on Service Employment in Developing Countries," *Economic Development and Cultural Change* 24:4 (July 1976), 765–786.

[4]The first estimate can be found in *Indicadores*, p. 23, and the second in *Compendio*, p. 52.

[5]*Manual de estadísticas básicas del Estado de Baja California*, vol. I, México, D.F.: Secretaría de Programación y Presupuesto, 1981, pp. 76–77.

[6]*Indicadores*, p. 17.

Table 1102

SHARES OF PRODUCTION SECTORS IN GDP AT FACTOR COST, FIFTY-SEVEN COUNTRIES GROUPED BY 1958 GDP PER CAPITA, ABOUT 1958

	Country Groups in Increasing Order of 1958 GDP per Capita							
	I	II	III	IV	V	VI	VII	VIII
Number of Countries	6	6	6	15	6	6	6	6
GDP per Capita	51.8	82.6	138	221	360	540	864	1,382
Shares of Major Sectors (%)								
Agriculture[1]	53.6	44.6	37.9	32.3	22.5	17.4	11.8	9.2
Industry	18.5	22.4	24.6	29.4	35.2	39.5	52.9	50.2
Mining and Quarrying	1.1	1.3	1.3	2.0	3.3	.7	2.2	2.4
Manufacturing	7.7	10.4	12.6	16.2	18.1	23.9	31.3	31.2
Construction	4.0	4.1	4.1	4.2	5.7	5.8	7.5	6.6
Electricity, Gas, and Water	.5	.7	.8	1.1	1.6	2.1	2.6	2.4
Transport and Communication	5.2	5.9	5.8	5.9	6.5	7.0	9.3	7.8
Services	27.9	33.0	37.5	38.3	42.3	43.1	35.3	40.6
Trade	12.8	11.8	13.5	15.3	14.9	13.5	11.3	14.2
Banking, Insurance, and Real Estate	.6	1.4	1.8	2.0	3.6	3.7	2.8	4.0
Ownership of dwellings	2.4	5.0	6.0	5.8	6.0	5.9	4.1	3.8
Public administration and defense	5.7	6.9	7.1	6.4	7.2	10.8	6.8	8.1
Other services	6.4	7.9	9.1	8.8	10.6	9.2	10.3	10.5

1. Includes agriculture, forestry, hunting, and fishing.

SOURCE: Simon Kuznets, *The Economic Growth of Nations*, table 12, p. 104.

Table 1103

SHARES OF PRODUCTION SECTORS IN LABOR FORCE, FIFTY-NINE COUNTRIES GROUPED BY 1958 GDP PER CAPITA ABOUT 1960, AND BAJA CALIFORNIA (BC), 1969[a]

	Country Groups in Increasing Order of 1958 GDP per Capita								
	I	II	III	IV	V	BC	VI	VII	VIII
GDP per Capita ($)	72.3	107	147	218	382	~	588	999	1,501
Shares of Major Sectors (%)									
Agriculture	79.6	63.9	66.2	59.6	37.8	24.0	21.8	21.8	11.6
Industry	9.9	15.2	16.0	20.1	30.2	30.1	40.9	47.2	48.1
Mining and Quarrying	1.2	1.2	.9	1.1	1.2	.5	.8	1.5	1.0
Manufacturing	5.7	7.5	9.0	11.6	17.4	19.6	24.2	28.3	9.7
Construction	1.4	2.9	2.8	3.9	6.0	6.1	8.5	8.3	8.5
Electricity, Gas, and Water	.2	.5	.6	.4	.9	.6	1.4	.8	1.4
Transport, storage, and communication	1.4	3.1	2.7	3.1	4.7	3.2	6.0	7.3	7.5
Services	10.4	20.9	17.8	20.3	32.0	45.9	37.3	33.9	40.3
Commerce	4.7	6.9	8.4	7.4	11.8	15.6	14.5	13.7	17.8
Services	5.7	14.0	9.4	12.9	20.2	30.4	22.8	20.2	22.5

a. Excludes unallocated labor.

SOURCE: Simon Kuznets, *The Economic Growth of Nations*, table 28, p. 200, and *Posibilidades*.

Table 1104

SECTORAL PRODUCT PER WORKER[1] AND RELATED MEASURES AT BENCHMARK VALUES OF GDP PER CAPITA, ABOUT 1960, AND BAJA CALIFORNIA, 1969

Major Sectors	Benchmark Values of 1958 GDP per Capital ($)					
	70 (1)	150 (2)	300 (3)	500 (4)	1,000 (5)	BC (6)
Agriculture (A)	.63	.63	.63	.65	.75	.42
Industry and Services (I&S)	2.53	1.64	1.32	1.16	1.05	1.19
Industry (I)	2.25	1.67	1.35	1.24	1.15	1.46
Manufacturing	1.75	1.58	1.28	1.20	1.15	1.35
Construction	3.23	1.42	1.04	.95	.85	.85
Transport, Storage and Communication, and Electricity, Gas and Water	4.18	2.15	1.75	1.60	1.38	2.70[a]
Services	2.80	1.61	1.29	1.06	.93	1.00
Trade	2.97	1.96	1.55	1.19	.94	.92
Services	2.65	1.39	1.13	.99	.92	1.05
Intersectoral Ratios						
(I+S)/A	4.02	2.60	2.10	1.78	1.40	2.83
S/I	1.24	.96	.96	.85	.81	.68
Trade/Services	1.12	1.41	1.37	1.20	1.02	.88

1. Sectoral product per worker (countrywide product per worker, excluding banking, insurance, and real estate, and income from ownership of dwellings = 1.00)

a. Baja California. GDP estimates include imputed value of services of privately owned motor vehicles in transport output.

SOURCE: S. Kuznets, *The Economic Growth of Nations*, table 31, p. 209, and *Posibilidades*.

Before one can attribute the high share of the services sector in employment to surplus labor, it is necessary to consider the factors that generate a high demand for services: the high degree of urbanization, which tends to raise the proportion of services in consumption expenditures, and the location of the population. Illustrating the importance of tourism is the fact that hotels, restaurants, and entertainment services accounted for one-eighth of GDP in 1965 and 1969 (table 1101). Furthermore, many people cross the border to purchase the services of doctors, dentists, beauty shops, auto mechanics, and auto body and paint shops, as well as to take advantage of Baja California's designation as a free trade zone, first granted to Tijuana and Ensenada in the early 1930s to encourage immigration and development of a region which for many years had been isolated from mainland Mexico. The success of this measure led to its adoption throughout the peninsula and in parts of the neighboring state of Sonora by the end of the decade. A natural economic interpretation of the structure of Baja California output and employment is that it simply reflects the comparative advantages of trading services for the relatively inexpensive foodstuffs and manufactured consumer goods found north of the border.

The External Sector

The economy of Baja California is extremely "open," as evidenced by the ratios of exports and imports to the GDP. Total regional exports equaled 71% and imports 69% of the estimated GDP in 1969. If trade with mainland Mexico is excluded, exports and imports amounted to 46% and 39% of the GDP in that year. Since the majority of Baja California's exports and a large share of imports are accomplished directly by persons moving across the border, the official foreign trade statistics do not reflect all of these transactions. For example, customs reported imports of 1.4 billion pesos and exports of 838 million in 1965. The input-output table estimates are 1.85 and 2.76 billion respectively for that year. The composition of trade with foreign countries estimated by the I-O method is presented in table 1106. The following eight categories accounted for 77.3% and 81.8% of foreign trade expenditures in 1965 and 1969: petroleum products; food and beverages; clothing and footwear; chemicals; iron and steel products; machinery and electrical equipment; transportation equipment and spare parts; miscellaneous industrial products. The second and third groups are composed mainly of consumer goods such

Table 1105

MALE AND FEMALE LABOR FORCE PARTICIPATION RATES BY AGE GROUPS, MEXICO AND BAJA CALIFORNIA (BC), 1970

(%)

PART I. Males

Age	Mexico	BC	Tijuana	Mexicali
12-14	12.8	5.5	5.0	5.9
15-19	49.9	37.3	38.6	35.7
20-24	79.6	74.0	74.8	72.4
25-29	90.6	86.7	86.2	86.6
30-34	93.2	90.7	90.4	90.9
35-39	94.3	92.3	91.6	93.3
40-44	93.9	91.8	91.2	92.6
45-49	93.9	91.1	90.4	92.2
50-54	92.3	88.9	88.1	90.0
55 and Over	79.9	73.3	70.1	75.3
Total	71.7	66.0	66.1	65.4

PART II. Females

Age	Mexico	BC	Tijuana	Mexicali
12-14	5.1	2.4	2.6	2.3
15-19	20.9	24.3	28.8	21.6
20-24	24.1	29.7	31.6	28.8
25-29	17.4	20.2	21.5	19.4
30-34	15.7	16.9	18.0	16.2
35-39	15.8	17.0	18.9	15.3
40-44	16.2	17.1	19.1	15.3
45-49	16.4	17.2	19.4	15.4
50-54	15.9	17.0	19.0	15.1
55 and Over	12.8	11.2	11.9	10.7
Total	16.4	18.1	20.0	16.7

SOURCE: *Indicadores socioeconómicos de las zonas fronterizas* (México, D.F.: Secretaría de Industria y Comercio, 1976), pp. 22 and 32 (hrerafter referred to as *Indicadores*).

as vegetables, dairy, and poultry products, underwear, men's and women's garments, and so on, while the fourth is a mixture of basic agricultural inputs (insecticides, fertilizers) and consumer goods (patent medicines, cosmetics, perfumes). Iron and steel comprehend laminates, tin plate and tin cans, hand tools, knives, pipe, and steel furniture. Industrial and agricultural machinery, motors, pumps, and home appliances fall into the next group. Transport equipment refers mainly to the purchase of used motor vehicles, and the miscellaneous category includes imports of ceramics, watches, jewelry, photographic equipment, and similar consumer goods which are major items of commerce with tourists due to the free zone provisions.

On the export side, eight major categories accounted for 93.2% and 92.3% of the totals in 1965 and 1969. These are: agricultural products; fish; petroleum products; food and beverages; miscellaneous products; hotel and restaurant services; amusement services; other services. The first category represents raw cotton and the second mainly lobster, abalone, and shrimp. Petroleum product exports reflect the sale of oil and fuel to foreign travelers while processed foods are composed of canned shellfish, fruits, and juices. Included in the miscellaneous category are imported ceramics, jewelry, and so forth, as well as domestically produced curios purchased by visitors. Hotels, restaurants, and amusements further reflect the expenditures of tourists, and the category "Other" represents the estimated value of remittances from nationals working across the border.

The data in table 1106 show the degree to which the state's economy has adapted to the advantages associated with its geographical location—a magnificent coastline and the Mexicali extension of Upper California's Imperial Valley within easy reach of the wealthy San Diego and Imperial counties to the north. Exports related to tourism accounted for roughly 40% to 50% of Baja California's foreign exchange earnings. Migrant workers' remittances contributed another quarter of these receipts during the late 1960s. From the standpoint of material welfare, the citizens of Baja California enjoy a standard of living far superior to the average for Mexico.

Levels of Welfare

Per capita income comparisons are difficult because of the lack of comparable data. Published estimates range from almost double to four times the national average.[7] Demographic and health statistics also display Baja California's advantages. For example, 1970 life expectancy in Baja California was 64.2 years for males and 70.8 years for females compared to 64 years for Mexico as a whole.[8] Child mortality rates of 6.3 per 1,000 live births in Baja California can be compared to Mexico's 7.5 per 1,000 (1974). Major causes of adult mortality in Mexico are enteritis and pneumonia, 87.5 and 90.0 respectively per 100,000 population. The corresponding rates in Baja California are 57.8 and 43.3. Baja California also fares better than Mexico in birth rates. Mexico has an estimated birth rate of 45.3 per 1,000; in Baja California, it is 40.7 per 1,000.[9] This, of course, does not deny a large gap between actual and desired standards of living.

---

[7]"Spotlight on Baja," *San Diego Economic Bulletin* (August 1975), p. 3, and Sergio Noriega Verdugo, "Aspectos económicos de Baja California, II," Banco Comercial de Baja California (Mexicali, B.C., 1974), mimeo.
[8]*Indicadores*, p. 14.
[9]Ibid.

Table 1106

COMPOSITION OF INTERNATIONAL TRADE, 1965 AND 1969

(%)

Category	Imports			Exports		
	1965	1969[a]	1969[b]	1965	1969[a]	1969[b]
Agricultural Products	4.25	2.03	1.52	20.27	12.69	9.26
Animal Products	2.81	2.71	2.03	.81	.86	.61
Forestry	.95	.94	.70	0	0	0
Fishing	0	0	0	2.19	2.12	1.51
Petroleum Products	6.08	6.08	4.55	2.65	2.85	2.04
Food, Beverages and Tobacco	11.58	20.86	15.63	8.10	8.89	6.35
Textiles	3.56	2.86	2.15	*	*	*
Clothing and Footwear	12.62	13.77	10.40	1.20	1.29	.92
Wood Products	1.00	1.12	.84	*	*	*
Paper Products	2.46	2.19	1.64	*	*	*
Publishing	*	*	*	*	*	*
Leather Goods	*	*	*	*	*	*
Rubber Goods	1.06	.79	.59	*	*	*
Chemicals	8.98	7.24	5.43	.60	.64	.46
Non-Metallic Metals	1.14	1.10	.83	*	*	*
Iron and Steel Products	6.68	6.07	4.55	*	*	*
Machinery and Electrical Equipment	16.76	15.33	11.48	*	*	*
Transport Equipment and Spares	8.83	7.55	5.66	*	*	*
Miscellaneous Industrial Products	5.78	4.76	3.56	8.37	9.02	6.44
Films	*	*	*	0	0	0
Transportation and Storage Service	.52	*	*	2.88	3.11	2.21
Hotel and Restaurant	1.52	1.26	.95	9.03	9.72	6.94
Amusements	.95	.72	.53	19.33	20.83	14.88
Other Services	.87	.72	.53	23.26	25.93	18.52
Banks, Insurance, and Real Estate	.77	.63	*	*	*	*
Total Value[1]	1,849.5	2,571.9	3,432.5	2,759.4	2,883.8	4,037.2

1. Millions of current pesos.

*Less than 5%.

a. Excludes imports and exports under the Border Industrialization Program.
b. Total trade under Border Industrialization Program.

SOURCE: *Posibilidades*, pp. 322, 323.

Table 1107 demonstrates the relative advantages of Baja California and some of the gaps to be filled by further development. The relative advantage of Baja California is apparent in all categories except those pertaining to the availability of water. The scarcity of water has been the greatest impediment to Baja California's development past and future. An indicator of the well-being of Baja California is the distribution of income per employed person (table 1108). Baja California and especially the border municipios enjoy a markedly more equitable distribution of income, as well as a generally higher income, than the average for Mexico. A major contributing factor is the absence of the subsistence type of agriculture which characterizes much of Mexico's interior. It is also reasonable to speculate that the predominance of service sector employment has increased the share of wages in total product, thus contributing to the relative size of the middle income groups.

Commercial Policy and the Free Trade Zone

As mentioned, the free zone privilege began experimentally in Tijuana and Ensenada in the early 1930s and was successful enough to be extended to all of Baja California and parts of Sonora by the end of the decade. Commercial policy for Mexico proper was initially directed toward the balance of payments after the wartime accumulation of reserves had been depleted, but, as in other Latin American nations, became increasingly oriented toward industrial protection and import substitution. Tariffs, import licensing, and quotas have been employed extensively to influence commodity trade, but the capital account has received liberal treatment. Undoubtedly, Mexico's geographic position has been a factor which has allowed, and to some extent required, the historic policy of free converti-

Table 1107

HOUSING CHARACTERISTICS, MEXICO AND BAJA CALIFORNIA, 1970

(%)

Housing	Mexico	Baja California
One room	40.1	23.1
Two rooms	28.9	29.4
Three rooms	13.8	20.9
Four or more rooms	17.1	26.6
Piped water (indoor)	38.7	41.7
Piped water (outdoor)	22.3	25.1
Running water in bathroom	31.8	33.3
Without sewers	58.0	56.6
Floors other than dirt	59.0	82.5
Gas or electricity for cooking	44.0	76.2
Electricity	58.9	79.0
Television	31.2	61.4

SOURCE: *Indicadores*, p. 18.

Table 1108

DISTRIBUTION OF MONTHLY INCOME AMONG THE EMPLOYED POPULATION, MEXICO AND BAJA CALIFORNIA, 1970

(%)

Monthly Income (in Pesos)	Mexico	Baja California	Mexicali	Tijuana
0 — 199	18.3	4.2	4.0	4.8
200 — 499	26.4	9.0	11.5	6.4
500 — 999	27.0	20.2	24.1	16.1
1,000 — 1,499	12.7	25.9	24.5	25.3
1,500 — 2,499	8.2	20.8	18.1	23.3
2,500 — 4,999	4.8	13.6	12.4	16.1
5,000 — 9,999	1.7	4.4	3.8	5.6
10,000 — and over	.9	1.9	1.6	2.4

SOURCE: *Indicadores*, pp. 21 and 31.

bility of the peso. Despite this relatively liberal attitude toward policy, the basic mercantilist-nationalist view of imports as lost domestic production has prevailed.

Baja California and the rest of La Frontera, as the border areas are called, received little attention during most of the postwar period, enjoying trading privileges but benefiting little from the government's development policies. In the 1960s, however, the elimination of the U.S. Bracero program and the sudden deterioration in the quality of Colorado River water flowing to the Mexicali Valley compelled the Mexican government to focus more attention on borderlands issues.

Spurred by the success of assembly industries in Asia, the Border Industrialization Program was established in 1966. Intended to provide jobs for those unemployed as a result of the termination of the Bracero program, the industrialization program granted U.S. firms free importation of equipment in order to assemble goods in Mexico for eventual sale in the United States. After a slow beginning, the program attracted 122 plants to Baja California by 1969, generating 1,153.4 million pesos in exports from 860.6 million pesos in imported inputs. The resulting 292.8 million pesos in net foreign exchange earnings for that year represent wages, salaries, and taxes.[10] Table 1106 shows the impact of the program on the composition of trade. Baja California's export surplus approximately doubled as a

---

[10]*Posibilidades*, p. 66.

consequence of the activities of the assembly industry. The Mexicali area especially welcomed the program as the decline of cotton was a severe blow to the local economy, but it had little direct impact on the employment of former farm workers as the majority of the labor force in these plants is female, a probable explanation for the relatively high LFP rate of women in Baja California (table 1105). The Mexican government undertook a major rehabilitation program in the Colorado River Irrigation District and entered into negotiations with the United States over the salinity problem.[11] The Mexicali investment project involved the lining and rebuilding of canals, leveling of fields, and consolidation of the irrigated area, as well as a major training effort to improve the use of water and propagate methods of controlling the bollworm.

This was the beginning of a new era for Baja California's relations with the federal government. The 1970 election brought into office the Echeverría administration, dedicated to regional development. Long overdue in view of the extreme geographic concentration of economic growth to date, the new policy orientation sought a better balance throughout the country. For Baja California this meant an attempt at the integration of the mainland and the border economies. The free trade privilege of Baja California has long been a sore point among Mexican industrial interests, which regard it as an avenue for the introduction of contraband from North American into their protected mainland markets. Furthermore, the rapid growth of population and income in Baja California had created a market which was relatively untapped by Mexican industry. Coupled with the politically popular view of trade policy referred to above, the new emphasis on regional development signaled a redirection of commercial policy as well as a greatly increased share of federal investment for Baja California. In the words of the then Secretary of Industry and Commerce:

> For many years the northern frontier zone has received little attention, possibly because it was thought that its singular characteristics made it difficult to apply the traditional development policies used in other regions. In this manner economic growth has occurred with an increasing loss of our frontier commerce; national industrialists have not considered the zone as part of their national market, taking for granted that it was impossible to compete with consumer goods from North America. On the other side of the picture, the acknowledged aggressiveness of the North American retailer and the modern services they have offered has led the consumers of this zone to become accustomed to sup-

plying themselves from the northern side of the border. The recapture of the frontier market for national producers has become one of the fundamental objectives of the policy of the President.[12]

The modifications subsequently introduced to stimulate regional development were not the first changes in the free trade policy applied to Baja California. In 1961, the National Frontier Program, aimed at encouraging import substitution in the border zone, was implemented. The Secretary of Finance was empowered to apply the regular mainland tariff and import taxes to imports into Baja California if similar articles were being produced there. Also, mainland products were extended protection from Baja California firms whose exports to the rest of the country were required to pay the duties on their imported inputs. As of 1969, some 300 products were subject to tariff in the free zone.[13] Many of the tariff classifications were so broad that they covered products that were neither produced in Baja nor imported from Mexico. Naturally this increased the volume of private imports due to residents shopping across the border. In addition to the tariffs under the control of the Secretary of Finance, the Secretary of Industry and Commerce was authorized to license imports of goods competing with national and local producers. Some 750 products were subjected to previous licensing in 1969, with the principal aim of reserving the local market for mainland products.[14] Local retailers often complained that the high price, poor quality, or irregular availability of these goods was harming their ability to compete with North American outlets, and occasionally the Secretary would allow these claims, providing additional import licenses on a temporary basis. In fact, the open nature of the economy made the usefulness of these restrictions questionable. Generally, it has been the retailer, not the consumer, whose welfare has suffered as a result of these measures. Protectionist policies are therefore subject to conflicting pressures. Mainland industries want the border closed in order to add Baja California to their market and to obstruct the flow of contraband, while commercial interests favor free trade. Baja California producers are in an intermediate position, hoping for protection for their goods and free trade in equipment and intermediate products as well as unrestricted rights to compete on the mainland.

Given this ticklish political dilemma, the new push toward Mexican economic integration is based on the granting of various subsidies in combination with the retention of the preexisting system of trade controls. Certain changes were made in the latter, namely an administrative decentralization of the Industry and Commerce quota sys-

---

[11] H. Brownell, "Desalinization and Mexican-American Relations," *American Journal of International Law*, no. 69, (April 1975), 255–271.

[12] Preface to *Estudio del desarrollo comercial de la frontera norte* (México, D.F.: Secretaría de Industria y Comercio, 1972).

[13] *Posibilidades*, p. 225.
[14] Ibid.

tem, and special treatment of spare parts and machinery. Furthermore, special items normally purchased across the border were granted free importation subject to a global quota in order to satisfy commercial interests. These provisions have had little impact in Baja California as it enjoys a more liberal trade regime than the rest of the border area. The subsidy programs are fairly complex but can be classified in three main groups according to their major objectives: (1) increased industrialization; (2) increased interchange of products between Baja California and the mainland; and (3) increased Mexicanization of commerce along the border.

Industrial Incentives

Border industries.—Several modifications to the border industry program have been made: exemption from the foreign investment regulations which require 51% Mexican participation (so that assembly firms may now be 100% foreign owned); assembly firms are automatically allowed to expand their operations as long as the existing ratio of Mexican ownership is retained; assembly plant import and export privileges are now available in most parts of Mexico; assembly plants in the border zone may be permitted to sell their products in Mexico (with payment of duties on inputs); the provision of the Constitution which forbids foreign ownership of property along the borders of the coastline was modified to allow foreigners to hold land rights in trust accounts for a period of thirty years; and, local firms which wish to subcontract assembly, finishing, etc. with foreign firms are allowed the same tariff exemptions on their inputs and equipment as the assembly plants.

New firms.—Baja California firms whose activities are new to the municipality or that use raw materials produced in the locality have been given a ten-year exemption from federal taxes on corporate income, stamp taxes, import tariffs on machinery and equipment, merchandiser's income tax, and accelerated depreciation for tax purposes on machinery and equipment. Similar tax exemptions of less than 100% apply to other new firms or to firms that increase their capacity in other parts of the country or for purposes different from the above.

Industrial parks.—A trust fund financed by an ad valorem export tax was established to encourage the development of industrial parks in Baja California and the other border zones.

Incentives to Integration

Freight subsidies.—The Secretary of Finance is authorized to grant a 25% reduction in freight charges to local firms buying primary inputs on the mainland; mainland exporters of manufactured goods are generally eligible for these subsidies, which are now available for their sales to Baja California as well; a 50% reduction in rail freight is available to finished consumers goods brought from the mainland to Baja California provided that (1) the products substitute for imports, (2) the products were selling for more than the foreign price, and (3) the resulting local price is inferior to the foreign price.

Relief from import duties.—Local firms are exempt from duties on inputs and equipment as long as their product substitutes for imports and has at least 40% local content (based on direct costs); exporting firms receive the same provisions plus the devolution of federal indirect taxes and the general export tax, if the local content is at least 50% of cost; mainland firms can also take advantage of these rebates if their product substitutes for imports in Baja California, that is, sales, are treated as exports.

Federal tax on merchandisers' incomes.—Exemptions are provided for Baja California firms bringing primary products into the state from the mainland and for any products which are of 100% national origin.

Shopping Centers

An intersecretarial committee has been established to promote the development of shopping centers similar to North American facilities (landscaping, parking, etc.) to encourage residents to shop on their side of the border. Provisions include: preferential import quotas (provided at least 50% of sales are of national products); exemption from import duties on machinery, materials and equipment for the construction, operation and maintenance of the center; warehousing facilities; accelerated depreciations; subsidized credit for construction and equipment purchases. (In comparison to the rest of the border areas, Baja California firms receive little benefit from the duty free provisions, due to the liberal trade regime in force there.)[15]

Balance of Payments

One would expect the incentive measures described to have an impact on income and employment in Baja California. It is difficult to determine whether this is the case in the absence of time series data. The Secretariat of Industry and Commerce claims the impact has been favorable. According to the Secretary of Finance, the amount of indirect taxes returned to mainland firms selling on the frontier rose from 16.1 million pesos in 1971 to 259.0 million in 1975, allowing an estimate of sales for the corresponding years of 177.1 and 1,942.5 million.[16] The data indicate,

---
[15]*Política económica fronteriza, 1971–1976* (México, D.F.: Secretaría de Industria y Comercio, 1976).
[16]Ibid, p. 38.

however, that the figure for tax rebates on frontier sales has been a constant 14% of the total rebates, suggesting that the sales estimate has been derived mechanically from all export sales subject to the same tax provisions, and is therefore of dubious validity.[17] Also supporting the Industry and Commerce position is the behavior of a Banco de México statistical series entitled Frontier Transactions. This series is based on dollar transactions handled by local banks along the border. All dollars received from local firms and individuals in cash or checks, except those representing receipts from commercial quantities of exports, are recorded in this account as inflow, while those dollars disbursed to individuals and firms are counted as outflow (again, dollars used for commercial-quantity imports are excluded). A comparison of these two totals provides an estimate of the balance of payments of the frontier zone for all transactions except those registered by customs. This balance of payments has been positive since 1950. During the period between 1965 and 1970, however, the outflow grew at an annual rate of 13.7% while the rate of growth of inflow was 11.3%. Consequently, the annual surplus grew at a rate of only 7.3%. The period encompassing the new programs (1970–1975) saw the surplus grow at an annual rate of 13.7%.

Although the behavior of the balance of frontier transactions is cited as an indicator of the success of the various programs designed to encourage industrial integration and import substitution, additional factors remain to be considered. First, from 1950 to 1975 the growth rates of inflow and outflow averaged 10.08% and 10.01% respectively. Consequently the positive balance has remained remarkably stable at three-eighths the value of inflow throughout the period. The absence of any trend casts some doubt on the impact of the new programs. Secondly, although one would expect the expenditures of North Americans in Baja California to appear in the inflow column, the peculiarities of the border economy may invalidate this assumption. The dollar has traditionally circulated in the border areas as a medium of exchange, convenience for the weekend visitor who would find it difficult to obtain pesos (the average visitor to Tijuana is estimated to spend only six hours). The residents have also found it easier to deal with one currency and one set of prices. Thus, prior to the 1976 devaluation, the dollar constituted as much as 98% of the circulating currency in Tijuana, and a similar, though smaller, proportion in other areas of the state depending on the frequency of transactions with tourists. In such a situation it is possible that some portion of the tourism receipts would return to the United States in the form of private imports without entering the local banking system. Furthermore,

the widespread use of the dollar would lead one to expect that the balances of residents and firms would be held in this currency. In fact, Baja California residents have been able to maintain dollar accounts at local banks. Growth of these deposits for transactions and speculative purposes makes it very difficult to infer anything about the success of import substitution from this series.

An additional factor adds to the difficulty of analyzing the balance of these frontier transactions. It was estimated that in the years 1965–1970 one-third of the inflow represented remittances of migrant workers. A large and unknown portion of the labor force works or has worked in the United States, although only a small portion is accounted for in the records of the U.S. Immigration and Naturalization Service. Popularly known as commuters, these individuals hold Alien Registration Receipt Cards (Form I-151), that is, they are lawful permanent residents who reside in Mexico but who work in the United States. As of March 31, 1971, there were 7,782 such persons coming to the United States regularly through San Ysidro, the entry point for Tijuana.[18] The corresponding number in August, 1976, was 15,714 (including 5,673 seasonal workers).[19] In addition to these commuters there are an unknown number of undocumented commuters, holders of the Nonresident Alien Mexican Border Crossing Cards (Form I-186) who take employment illegally upon crossing the border. Then, of course, there are the "wetback" or *alambrista* workers who enter illegally and work illegally as well. By all indications their number has increased substantially in recent years. The number of undocumented Mexican nationals discovered by the authorities in California is shown in table 1109.

Table 1109

DEPORTABLE MEXICAN NATIONALS LOCATED IN CALIFORNIA, 1970–76

Fiscal Year	N
1970	107,939
1971	114,652
1972	134,551
1973	214,673
1974	181,770
1975	304,356
1976	342,223

SOURCE: United States Department of Justice, Immigration and Naturalization Service, Western Region, San Pedro, California (October 1976).

---

[17]*Indicadores*, p. 87.

[18]Sergio Noriega, "Tijuana y su mercado" (September 1972), mimeo.

[19]U.S. Department of Justice, Immigration and Naturalization Service, Western Region, San Pedro, California (October 1976).

As many individual Mexican nationals have relocated several times, and the efforts of the Border Patrol may vary in intensity, it is difficult to relate this number to a total, but it seems to indicate a significant increase in the number of persons crossing the border in search of work. In March of 1976, the Immigration and Naturalization Service estimated the total number of Mexican nationals in California as 1,560,000 to 1,728,000, of which an estimated 1,050,000 to 1,160,000 were employed. Many of those employed send money to Mexico as do many of the one million Mexican nationals legally resident in California. The resulting inflow of dollars must be substantial, but there is no way at present to estimate the amount reaching Baja California.

In addition to remittances, movements on capital accounts could provide a significant source of dollars. High interest rates have presumably attracted savings from across the border. What may be more important is that there has evidently been a great deal of real investment in construction along the coast. It is not clear that the statistics of frontier transactions reflect this flow of real investments.

Given the inflationary trends of the recent past—the purchasing power of the peso has been declining relative to that of the dollar—the surplus of the balance of payments could be expected to have become ever more negative. That this has apparently not occurred may attest to the success of the import substitution policy. The increased growth rate of the surplus is the result of a decline in the rate of growth of the outflow. The relative importance of the external sector is apparently declining ("apparently" is appropriate here because there is no information on domestic activity for comparison) and in real terms it most assuredly is declining, characteristic of an import substitution policy. However, in the absence of further information on the composition of the various transactions recorded in the overall balance, it seems best to view the impact of the subsidies and related policies as an open question.

Summary

The highly urbanized (85.5%) and rapidly expanding (7.2% annually) population of Baja California is mainly the result of the migration of poorer Mexican citizens hoping to share in the relatively higher standard of living to be found along the California border. The data on production and employment show that the citizens of Baja earn these higher incomes largely by trading their services for consumer goods readily available in the mass markets of the United States. This takes place through the provision of services to visitors coming from California (one-eighth of GDP is derived from hotels, restaurants, and entertainment services alone) to enjoy the coastal amenities and take advantage of the duty-free shops, from employment in the border assembly industries (which raised Baja California's exports by almost 40% as early as 1969), and from working legally and illegally in California and other states (their remittances have been estimated to account for roughly 20%–25% of export receipts). The outcome is an economic structure unique in comparison to economies of similar per capita income levels. Forty-six percent of GDP originates in commerce and services and only 24% in agriculture, where relative productivity is abnormally low; and there is basically no heavy industry at all.

While the population continues to surge, the aridity, salinity, and general topography of the frontier indicate that agriculture is not likely to provide much additional employment, although expansion of intensive farming of vegetable and tree crops for export and import substitution can help to bring the productivity of the rural population closer to the average. Thus urbanization must be expected to continue and the population will therefore look to manufacturing and service employment as a source of income. Yet development in manufacturing has lagged in comparison to other areas of the world, largely because of the difficulty of controlling imports. On the other hand, the openness of the regional economy is a major reason for the relatively high level of well-being which originally attracts the population. It seems that development must continue along roughly the same paths of the recent past, relying on services, assembly of goods for re-export, and probably on an increasing flow of remittances from the United States.

Unfortunately, this scenario implies that the pace of development will continue to be dependent on the health of the U.S. and California economies. The major problem for Baja California recently is that it has been subjected to the conflicting macroeconomic policies of Mexico and the United States. Mexico's financial problems and the drastic fall of the peso in relation to the dollar have had a severe impact. The region's open economy leaves almost no leeway for devaluation to stimulate a reallocation of resources from "home" goods to export- and import-competing industries, which is supposed to be the beneficial long-term structural result of an increased price of foreign exchange. Furthermore, the financial integration with California accompanying this openness has meant that many balance sheets were heavy with dollar liabilities unmatched by dollar assets.[20] Consequently, devaluation is a strong deflationary impulse along the border. Although part of the

---

[20]Only anecdotal information is available on this point. For example, Francisco Pinchetti has written that frontier residents held two billion dollars in debt to U.S. banks and retailers in early 1982. Francisco Ortiz Pinchetti, "La Frontera, hambrienta en un aislamiento que es un jauja de especuladores," *Proceso* (October 11, 1982).

shock is absorbed on the other side by those businesses relying on the border trade, the greater hardship remains in Mexico, where prices are set in terms of dollars (and thus respond almost proportionally to devaluation), while peso wages and salaries react more slowly. Most Baja California firms are placed in such a tight cash flow position following devaluation that they are unable to respond to the temporary fall in real wages. By the time rising nominal expenditures have enabled them to regain normal liquidity, this same rise of nominal income has offset the previous decline in real wages. Devaluation does allow mainland firms to expand their markets in Baja California, as their costs are slower to react, but, in contrast, regional exports to the mainland are likely to diminish as mainland firms exploit their new cost advantages over the local products.

Ideally, from an economic standpoint, Baja California's financial system should be completely and permanently integrated with that of California to allow the flow of cheap labor (in dollar terms) into the regional economy to be matched with a flow of inexpensive capital from the United States to complete the structural integration with the larger economy to the North. Politically, however, this would rapidly result in a de-Mexicanization of the capital stock as the foreign-owned facilities would grow much faster than the domestic. Such a "colonization" of Baja's economy would surely be unacceptable. Thus, for the short to medium term, the economy will be subject to the pressure of a growing population, shortages of domestic capital, and a state government increasingly unable to meet the increasing demands for basic services which the growth of the population implies.[21] Unable to separate itself from either the U.S. or the mainland economies, Baja California must somehow manage to stay afloat until financial stability is regained in Mexico.

---

[21]With the increase in federal government attention to Baja under the presidency of Echeverría, the state government had been able to expand social services rapidly but the crises of 1976 slowed progress greatly. For example, the proportion of primary school age children attending school had been increasing, but from 1974 to 1977 the increase in the number of students just barely surpassed the increase in the number of children not attending. The current crisis is clearly going to result in much greater fiscal stringency at both the federal and state levels. *Manual de estadísticas básicas*, vol. 2, p. 439.

12

The Gap Between Theoretical Modeling and the Application of These Models to the U.S.–Mexican Border Economy

Jerry R. Ladman

Peter L. Reich, ed., *Statistical Abstract of the United States–Mexico Borderlands.*
Statistical Abstract of Latin America Supplement 9 (Los Angeles: UCLA Latin
American Center Publications, University of California, 1984).

The economy of the U.S.-Mexican border region is unique to both countries. It is characterized by a number of contiguous economic regions surrounding population centers located on each side of the border and separated by an international boundary. Often, these regions have grown up around an economic base derived from natural resources, such as mining or irrigated agriculture. In other cases, they have resulted mainly from points of trade or tourism. Because of their relative isolation from the main economies of the two countries as well as a long history of open economic relations between the two nations, including relatively unrestricted flows of products and resources, the contiguous regional border economies have grown accustomed to considerable economic interchange. Consequently, because of these linkages, events affecting economic conditions on one side of the border have important impacts, not only on that country's border region but also on that of the other.

In 1979 I elaborated a theoretical model, the twin-city multiplier, which describes the interdependence arising from the economic interchange between contiguous border regions and shows how economic factors, either endogenous or exogenous to the border, affect both regions. Such models serve to conceptualize and describe the nature of the interdependent economic relationships in the contiguous regions and, if applied, would be useful in predicting changes in the two economies, were there to be changes in economic policies and/or conditions. There have been few attempts to apply the models, however, principally due to the large costs and difficulties of obtaining adequate and timely data. In this chapter, I will briefly review the model, examine the problems in applying it, and argue the need for the collection of adequate data.

The Model

As originally developed by Ladman[1] and refined by Ladman and Duffy,[2] the model combines regional and foreign-trade multiplier analysis to show the equilibrium level of economic activity in two contiguous border regional economies, A and B, as a function of the levels of autonomous spending in both and taking into account the linkages between the two economies which arise from induced spending. The model shows how the two economies will adjust to changes in either the levels of autonomous spending or factors causing induced spending in either region. Furthermore, the model can be used as an analytical framework to examine the historical economic development of a two-country border region.

Autonomous spending in A or B can arise from many sources. Typical examples are government expenditures on projects, private sector investment in business, and the production of goods and services for export from the region. Because of induced spending within either region, autonomous spending in A (B) gives rise to an equilibrium level of income, $Y_A(Y_B)$, which is larger than the original autonomous spending. This is due to the direct multiplier effect in the region, which depends on what proportion of income earned in the region tends to be re-spent directly in the region.

Because there are two contiguous regions, where income earners from one tend to spend a portion of their incomes in the second, there is another multiplier, the cross multiplier, that will influence Y_A and Y_B. When incomes in $A(B)$ rise or fall due to a change in the level of autonomous spending in $A(B)$, there will be a positive or negative impact on $Y_B(Y_A)$ as purchases in $B(A)$ by residents of $A(B)$ rise or fall accordingly. Since a portion of the incomes earned as a result of these purchases in $B(A)$ will be re-spent in the other economy, there will be rises or declines in both Y_A and Y_B due to a cross multiplier effect.

Therefore, the total level of Y_A and Y_B will depend both upon the size of initial autonomous expenditure in A and/or B as well as the sizes of the direct and cross multipliers in A and B. The equilibrium values of Y_A and Y_B are shown in Equations (1) and (2).

$$Y_A = D_A S_A + R_A S_B \qquad (1)$$

$$Y_B = R_B S_A + D_B S_B \qquad (2)$$

In these equations $D_A(D_B)$, $R_A(R_B)$, and $S_A(S_B)$ correspond to the direct multiplier, cross multiplier, and the sum of autonomous expenditure in $A(B)$ respectively.

The two equations can be used to show the effects of any change, or combination of changes, in the level of autonomous expenditures on the levels of Y_A and Y_B. For example, if there were an increase (decrease) in autonomous spending ΔS_A in region A the impact on both re-

---

[1] Jerry R. Ladman, "The Economic Interdependence of Contiguous Border Cities: The Twin City Multiplier," *The Annals of Regional Science* 13(1) (March, 1979).

[2] Jerry R. Ladman and Michael K. Duffy, "Intercambio económico en el area fronteriza mexicana-norteamericana: comercio y turismo," *Estudios fronterizos* (Mexico City: ANUIES, 1981), pp. 185–206.

gions—ΔY_A and ΔY_B—would be shown as in Equation (3). In a similar fashion the effect of a ΔS_B could be represented.

$$\Delta Y_A = D_A(\Delta S_A)$$

$$\Delta Y_B = R_B(\Delta S_A) \tag{3}$$

The above equations are presented in aggregate form. When disaggregated, they become much more complex, as shown in Equations (4)–(9).[3]

$$S_A = \bar{c}_A + \bar{I}_A + \bar{G}_A + (\bar{m}_B^A + \bar{X}_A^R) - (\bar{m}_A^B + \bar{m}_A^R) +$$

$$[(m_A^B + m_A^R) - c_A]\bar{T}_A - m_B^A \bar{T}_{B'} \tag{4}$$

$$S_B = \bar{c}_B + \bar{I}_B + \bar{G}_B + (\bar{m}_A^B + \bar{X}_B^R) - (\bar{m}_B^A + \bar{m}_B^R) +$$

$$[(m_B^A + m_B^R) - c_B]\bar{T}_B - m_A^B \bar{T}_{A'} \tag{5}$$

$$D_A = \frac{s_B + (m_B^A + m_B^R)}{[s_A + (m_A^B + m_A^R)][s_B + m_B^A + m_B^R)] - m_A^B m_B^{A'}} \tag{6}$$

$$R_A = \frac{m_B^A}{[s_A + (m_A^B + m_A^R)][s_B + (m_B^A + m_B^R)] - m_A^B m_B^{A'}} \tag{7}$$

$$R_B = \frac{m_A^B}{[s_A + (m_A^B + m_A^R)][s_D + (m_D^A + m_D^R)] - m_A^B m_B^{A'}} \tag{8}$$

$$D_B = \frac{s_A + (m_A^B + m_A^R)}{[s_A + (m_A^B + m_A^R)][s_B + (m_B^A + m_B^R)] - m_A^B m_B^{A'}} \tag{9}$$

In this form letters carrying a "bar" over them denote autonomous spending. For region A, $\bar{c}_A$ represents consumption, $\bar{I}_A$ investment, $\bar{G}_A$ government expenditure, $\bar{m}_B^A$ export sales from A to B, $\bar{X}_A^R$ export sales from A to the rest of the world (defined to be outside A or B), $\bar{m}_A^B$ purchases of imports from B to A, $\bar{m}_A^R$ import purchases from the rest of the world to A, and $\bar{T}_A$ taxes in A. There are corresponding variables for region B.

There are behavioral parameters in the model which provide the link between autonomous spending and the equilibrium levels of income. These parameters determine the size of the multipliers because they give rise to induced spending. In the model they are those variables without a "bar," and correspond to marginal propensities. For region A, c_A represents the marginal propensity to consume, s_A the marginal propensity to save, m_A^B the marginal propensity to import to B from A, and m_A^R the marginal propensity to import from R to A. There are corresponding variables for region B.

If one or several of these parameters were to change, there would be a corresponding impact on Y_A and Y_B. The model can be used to show the effects.

Problems in Applying the Model

The model, if applied, would offer considerable potential in showing the impact of new economic policies or changed economic conditions that result in new autonomous expenditure or change in parameters, in either or both A and B, on Y_A and Y_B. There are, however, two important problems.

The first is that the model is expressed in real, not monetary, terms. When the model was developed, this aspect was not such an important shortcoming because the exchange rate between the U.S. and Mexican currencies was virtually constant. However, this has changed in recent years, especially since 1982, when the exchange rate has fluctuated considerably. Changes in the relative prices of goods in the two regions will affect the marginal propensities for residents of A and B to undertake induced consumer spending in their region as well as their imports from the other region and the rest of the world. Likewise, price changes may also impact on the marginal propensity to save. Moreover, these changes may impact on autonomous expenditures such as those of tourists, investment in manufacturing, and government investments or transfer payments.

The model could be adjusted to take these changes into account. To do so, however, would make it more complex and require detailed knowledge about the relationships between changes in relative prices and those of induced consumption spending, savings, and autonomous expenditures. Moreover, this knowledge would be expensive and time consuming to obtain.

The second problem is obtaining adequate data. It would be necessary to monitor and specify changes in autonomous expenditure. For new projects that involve a fixed investment and payroll this should not be difficult. However, for autonomous expenditures emanating from production for export, tourism, or import-export activities, the amounts will depend upon a number of factors exogenous to the regions, but which must be considered in estimating the amount of such expenditures in the two regions. This would require knowledge of and data about these relationships and how they affect expenditure in the two regions.

---

[3]The reader is referred to Ladman and Duffy, "Intercambio económico," for a complete elaboration of the model.

A more serious aspect of the problem is estimating the model's parameters that account for induced spending, for example, all the marginal propensities. The model assumes several marginal propensities for both A and B. There is virtually no accurate way to obtain this information other than through sizable sample surveys of both populations. Done correctly, the sample should be stratified to account for different social and income classes. Such surveys are time consuming and very costly. Moreover, because of the changes in relative prices, they must be updated regularly to take into account the effect on the parameters of changes in the exchange rate. In addition, structural changes in the two economies, including revised tax laws and government regulations—such as exchange controls and others affecting imports and exports—as well as the relative availability or quality of goods, will cause changes in the parameters and must be dealt with.

Finally, it must be realized that there are a number of contiguous border regional economies. Each is different from the other in terms of structure and economic base. The sources of autonomous expenditure and the magnitude of the parameters will vary. Therefore, if the parameters of the model were estimated for a given region they would not necessarily be transferable to other regions. To be meaningful for the whole border, the model would have to be applied independently in each region, which would be a very costly process.

Conclusion

The above model and others, such as input-output models, can be useful in describing the economies of contiguous border regions. They are important as conceptual frameworks in understanding the complexity and interrelatedness of the two economies. However, the application of such models to predict changes in economic activity resulting from new policies or economic conditions requires considerable data, which are very costly and time consuming to obtain. Moreover, they must be regularly updated in order to be valid.

The lack of adequate data and the cost of obtaining them are the reasons for the existing gap between the theory of the border economy and the applications of that theory to show the quantitative impact of new or proposed economic policies and conditions on both of the contiguous regions. As the contiguous economies are rapidly becoming larger and more important to both nations, it would be very useful to be able to predict the impact of economic policies and conditions on the regions. However, to do so would require significant expenditure to obtain adequate data. It is hoped that the recent establishment of border data banks at San Diego State University, the Centro de Estudios Fronterizos del Norte de México (CEFNOMEX), and elsewhere will facilitate the collection of information on a regular and continuing basis so that the gap between theory and application will be eliminated.

13

Industrial Technology Transfer for Borderlands Development: The Need for a U.S.–Mexican Data Base

Martin E. Rosenfeldt

Industrial technology transfer for regional development is an issue which has assumed particular significance in the U.S.–Mexican borderlands during the last decade. Obvious differences in economic activities "across the Rio Grande," differences in the standard of living, per capita income, levels of employment, and development of the regional infrastructures provoke inquiries into the reasons for such socioeconomic disparities. An identification and evaluation of selected symbiotic co-variate relationships in terms of industrial technology transfer will aid in the promotion of regional development in the U.S.–Mexican borderlands.

Regional Borderlands Symbiosis

One of the primary objectives of the research project described here was to identify socioeconomic co-variates influencing regional development of the McAllen/Reynosa borderlands during the last decade. Economic activity takes place in a bicultural environment and is strongly influenced by dynamic processes involving commercial and sociopolitical interaction. The marked increase in the region's economic development during the past decade is seen as a natural outcome of a symbiotic relationship between the adjoining U.S. and Mexican borderlands. Until the recent economic crisis in Mexico, labor and capital inputs have been able to circulate with relative ease with the aid of U.S. and Mexican economic forces. Traditional geopolitical boundaries and tariff and cross-border trade restrictions which typically tend to limit the economic development of border cities did not appreciably influence the symbiotic interaction of either border region. The assumption was made, therefore, that the influx of industrial development and industrial technology into the Lower Rio Grande Valley and Reynosa is a result of strong symbiotic relationships which are essentially economic. In addition, strong cultural symbiotic relationshps exist in the McAllen SMSA/Reynosa region due to the high percentage (81.3%) of population of Spanish-speaking origin living in the area.[1]

In the survey of regional industrial development and technology inflow in the Lower Rio Grande region, selected economic variables were identified and quantified. This task was complicated by the fact that data obtained from public and private sector sources were frequently sketchy and incomplete, or unavailable. Nonetheless, ten co-variates were identified and used in the interpretation of symbiotic relationships of the industrial sectors of the McAllen SMSA/Reynosa borderlands.

The field research addressed the following topics: 1. economic and industrial development of the Reynosa region; 2. economic and industrial development of the Mc-Allen SMSA; 3. identification of regional co-variates (inference on industrial technology transfer); and 4. recent economic development.

Socioeconomic variables, which are indicators for industrial development and identified as co-variates in the selected border regions, were population, pedestrian and vehicular border crossings, and, in the manufacturing sector, employment, taxable payroll, value added, gross domestic product, number of business units, per capita value added, and per capita gross domestic product. Summaries of the Reynosa/McAllen SMSA co-variate analysis and cross-regional co-variate analysis in terms of comparative percentages for the years 1970 and 1975 are shown in tables 1300, 1301, 1302, and 1303.[2] Although the absolute values of the selected variables vary, their comparative growth rates are indicative of co-variation, thus establishing the validity of the hypothesis of regional symbiosis.

Essentially symbiotic economic relationships emerge from a comparison of selected demographic and economic variables for 1970 and 1975 in the McAllen SMSA/Reynosa region. Field research to collect statistical and qualitative evidence on regional development through

---

AUTHOR'S NOTE: This chapter is based on field research conducted in the U.S.–Mexican borderlands. See also Martin E. Rosenfeldt and Joe M. Brocato, "Industrial Technology Transfer for Regional Development in the Lower Valley/Reynosa Borderlands." Paper presented at the annual meeting of the North American Economics and Finance Association, New York, December 1982.

---

[1] 1980 Census of Population, Volume I, Chapter B. *General Population Characteristics*. Part 45, Texas. U.S. Department of Commerce, U.S. Printing Office, Washington, D.C., August 1982. SMSA is the acronym for Standard Metropolitan Statistical Area, a county or group of counties containing at least one city having a population of 50,000 or more.

[2] Martin E. Rosenfeldt and Joe M. Brocato, "Industrial Technology Transfer for Regional Development in the Lower Valley/Reynosa Borderlands." Paper presented at the annual meeting of the North American Economics and Finance Association, New York, December 1982. Table IV.1; p. 24, tables IV.2, IV.3, and IV.4.

Table 1300

REYNOSA/McALLEN SMSA CO-VARIATE ANALYSIS: SUMMARY OF ECONOMIC INDICATOR GROWTH RATES, 1970 AND 1975[a]

Co-variate	Totals 1970	Totals 1975	Five Year Growth Rate (%)
Population (N)			
Reynosa (17)	150,186	180,043	19.4
McAllen (18)	71,496	76,753	7.4
Employment in Manufacturing (N)			
Reynosa	1,760	2,770	57.4
McAllen	2,861	3,945	37.9
Taxable Payroll in Manufacturing (US)			
Reynosa	1,436,000	5,984,000	316.7
McAllen	13,728,000	25,931,000	88.9
Value-Added in Manufacturing (US)			
Reynosa	2,831,600	19,800,000	599.3
McAllen	10,396,320	75,200,000	623.3
Gross Domestic Product in Manufacturing (US)			
Reynosa	6,543,760	86,090,000	1215.6
McAllen	19,541,840	190,800,000	876.4
Business Units in Manufacturing (N)			
Reynosa	304	289	−4.9
McAllen	123	131	6.5
Total Border Crossings, North and South (N)			
Pedestrian (19)	6,504,000	9,916,000	52.5
Vehicular	2,132,000	3,160,000	48.2

a. PEMEX figures not included. All monetary amounts in current dollars.

Table 1301

REYNOSA/McALLEN SMSA CO-VARIATE ANALYSIS, 1970 AND 1975: CROSS-REGIONAL CO-VARIATES IN TERMS OF COMPARATIVE PERCENTAGES[a]

Co-variates	Reynosa/McAllen, 1970 (%)	Reynosa/McAllen, 1975 (%)
Population	210.1	234.6
Employment — Manufacturing	61.5	70.2
Taxable Payroll — Manufacturing	10.5	23.1
Value-added in Manufacturing	27.2	26.3
Per capita value added — Manufacturing	13.0	11.2
GDP — Manufacturing	33.5	45.1
Per capita GDP — Manufacturing	15.9	19.2
Business Unit — Manufacturing	247.2	220.6
Total border crossings[b]		
Pedestrians and passengers	100.0	100.0
Vehicles	100.0	100.0

a. PEMEX figures not included.
b. Reynosa/McAllen, same.

Development of Data

Table 1302

REYNOSA/McALLEN SMSA CO-VARIATE ANALYSIS, 1970 AND 1975: PER CAPITA VALUE ADDED BY MANUFACTURING[a]

(%)

	1970	1975	5-Year Growth Rate
Reynosa	18.8	109.9	484.6
McAllen	145.4	979.8	573.9

a. PEMEX figures not included.

Table 1303

REYNOSA/McALLEN SMSA CO-VARIATE ANALYSIS, 1970 AND 1975: PER CAPITA GROWTH RATE OF GDP IN MANUFACTURING[a]

(%)

	1970	1975	5-Year Growth Rate
Reynosa	43.4	478.2	1,001.8
McAllen	273.3	2,486.0	809.6

a. PEMEX figures not included.

industrial technology transfer (as demonstrated by manufacturing-related economic co-variate analysis) was complicated by difficulties in locating comparable and accurate data on both sides of the U.S.–Mexican borderlands region.

Interpretation of Field Research

Implicit in the research project are three hypotheses: 1. regional development is achieved on a basis of industrial technology transfer; 2. symbiotic relationships exist between the United States and Mexico borderland populations in their socioeconomic existence; and 3. this symbiotic relationship can be visualized (if not measured) by interpreting selected socioeconomic co-variates.

To gain firsthand insight into data availability and data collection techniques which describe industrial technology transfer techniques, related private and public sector service agencies and educational institutions were contacted in the Lower Rio Grande Valley, McAllen, and Reynosa, as well as the Office of the Governor in Austin (see appendix A). In interviews with persons responsible for data compilation, research, and publication, information was obtained on agencies involved in statistical data retrieval, and the nature and type of socioeconomic variables monitored on both sides of the border were researched. Information was gathered on the extent to which data were available, and on dissemination efforts.

Significant differences in the task responsibilities of data collection, availability, and publication on either side of the border were found. These differences are undoubtedly based on the different sociopolitical systems of the United States and Mexico. While the developed economy of the United States provides the entrepreneurial motivation of mostly private Texan business activities to explore business opportunities in the border region, this is generally not the case in the Mexican border region. Mexico is a developing nation with a highly uneven income distribution and, compared to that of the United States, low per capita income.[3] Its economy is centrally controlled by the Mexican federal government. Since the recent nationalization of the private banking system, more than 80% of the Mexican gross national product is produced by state owned or partially controlled businesses. Notwithstanding this high government participation, the private sector has thus far been considered the "steam engine" of the Mexican economy.

Although the economic activities of the McAllen SMSA were mainly agricultural until the 1960s, it has since attracted an influx of commercial, industrial, and tourist-related businesses. This rapid regional development has to be attributed partially to the participation of Mexican residents frequenting business establishments in the McAllen SMSA. Although the recent severe economic crisis in Mexico and resulting scarcity of foreign currency have drastically reduced this commercial symbiosis in the U.S.–Mexican borderlands, expectations are that commercial activities will gradually return to normal as the country regains its economic capacities, although it will probably have different commercial priorities.[4]

Simultaneously with the increasing economic development of the McAllen SMSA, the Mexican government initiated its Border Industrialization Program to provide employment opportunities for the rapidly growing Mexican borderland population. Industrial development of the Reynosa region was promoted by the installation of U.S. assembly plants on the Mexican side of the border. Since the initiation of this program more than 630 plants with about 130,000 Mexican employees have been established along the Mexican side of the border, from Matamoros to Tijuana. The resulting transfer of technologies through the establishment of labor-intensive, foreign-owned industries has

---

[3]Raymond Vernon and Louis T. Wells, Jr., *Economic Environment of International Business,* 3d ed. (Englewood Cliffs, N.J.: Prentice-Hall, Inc., 1981), pp. 130–131.

[4]Martin E. Rosenfeldt and Ted Halatin, "Marketing Strategies in a Changing Environment: Emphasis on U.S.-Mexican Businesses." Paper presented at the Southwestern Marketing Association, Houston, Texas, March 1983.

contributed both to the Mexican balance of payments and to the regional development of the areas which benefited from initiatives by the Mexican government and U.S. private enterprise.

On the Texan side of the U.S.–Mexican borderlands, statistical data and qualitative information on ongoing programs which influence the economy of the border region were obtained principally from the following sources: McAllen and Rio Grande Valley Chambers of Commerce, Texas Industrial Commission, McAllen Industrial Board, Office of the Governor of Texas 2000 Project, Census of Population, and Census of Manufacturers of the U.S. Department of Commerce. The Bureaus of Business and Economic Research at The University of Texas at Austin and the Pan American University at Edinburg, Texas, and the Institute of International Trade at Laredo State University produced miscellaneous statistical data on borderlands economic and trade activities. Socioeconomic and business data from these sources represent a wide spectrum of information retrieval. The thrust of research activities by these agencies depends upon their particular objectives in information collection. Undoubtedly, there are other regional agencies and institutions which collect and disseminate statistical data on socioeconomic and industrial borderlands activities depending upon their own research interests. As a regional agency coordinating these research activities and data collection does not seem to exist, duplications occur. As a result, the data retrieved for this project represent socioeconomic statistics available for studies of the U.S.–Mexican borderlands.

The field research to obtain statistical data in the Reynosa region, which would be helpful in the study of regional industrial development, proved to be significantly different from similar research in the United States. Contacts with agencies representing private enterprise, such as the Mexican Chamber of Commerce of Reynosa, confirmed that business activities in this region are centralized and government controlled. Private sector initiative in the Lower Rio Grande Valley produced a wealth of statistical information to assist Texan companies in their business and strategy planning. There were no such data found in Reynosa (see appendix B). Business statistics appeared to be available in relation to socioeconomic data compiled from Mexican census figures (see appendix C). Even Mexican private sector surveys, such as the Planeación Arquitectónica PLAR, S.C.'s "Estudio socio-económico y análisis de mercado," a 217-page study, contained socioeconomic information derived principally from government sources. However, large Mexican business firms have compiled business-related studies, market surveys, and similar statistical material. Mexican business practices do not seem to include the dissemination of "company secrets" for the benefit of the business community.

Analysis of Data Limitations

One of the primary objectives of the research was the identification of socioeconomic variables which can be used to indicate the extent of industrial technology transfer in the symbiotic regional development of the McAllen SMSA/Reynosa borderlands. The co-variate indicators (see table 1301) give evidence of similar conditions and hypothesized mutually interdependent socioeconomic development through industrial activities during 1970–1975.

Socioeconomic and business studies in which time series values of selected variables have to be gleaned are only as valid as the statistical data collected. The number of business studies which can be conducted in a region is high and, for all practical purposes, indeterminate. The provision of socioeconomic and business data by public and private service agencies will, therefore, have to be restricted to generally applicable statistical information. Because of this restriction, business research frequently has to utilize related statistical data that do not mirror a particular phenomenon or hypothesis. The more extensive and in-line time series coincide with the research objective, the more useful will be related deductions, analogies, or extrapolations.

Data Sources

Socioeconomic data and statistics to evaluate regional industrial development are composed of specific information. Such data can be found quantified in the form of statistics and economic and business variables, which are measured and recorded in time series. Related information can also be qualitative, describing ongoing or projected programs of private or publicly inspired industrial technology transfer which may eventually promote the economic development of a region. These programs form part of business or government strategies of private or public enterprise. Locating related information presented considerable difficulties. Information on such programs and projects is dispersed. No centralized public or private enterprise was found which serves as a clearinghouse for projects involving industrial technology transfer in the McAllen SMSA borderlands. Neither the Office of the Governor nor regional representatives of the private sector appear to have included the expansion of U.S. industrial business activities into the Reynosa border region in their work program. Apparently insufficient knowledge of Mexican business legislation by U.S. business entrepreneurs prevents them from entering into joint ventures with Mexican partners in the Reynosa border region. Here, symbiotic interaction would enable businessmen on both sides of the border to enter the potentially lucrative Mexican market by making use of the many Mexican fiscal incentives to promote the industrial development of the border region. One notable exception found was the McAllen Industrial Board. It was observed, however, that the promotion of twin-plant and *maquiladoras* programs rested in the hands of a few capable persons who acted within a framework of incomplete information and regional isolation.[5] Federal and state initiatives to promote regional development through concerted industrial expansion across the border were not observed.

In the Reynosa region, a somewhat reverse situation was observed. While in the Lower Rio Grande Valley private sector service organizations actively collect economic and business-related data, and publish the compiled information, in Reynosa the private sector appeared to be remarkably absent. On the other hand, various public sector agencies have installed offices and provided evidence of border industrialization programs for the extended Reynosa border region (see appendixes).

Statistical data documenting regional, industrial development can be presented in two categories: socioeconomic data and business indicators, such as sales, financial, production, and marketing information (see also appendix B). Public sector data, such as the Mexican Census of Population and Census of Manufacturers, provide socioeconomic statistics, consistent with the availability of U.S.-related data. Business data consistent with those published in the *Statistical Data Book* of the Rio Grande Valley of Texas were not found in Reynosa. On the other hand, various detailed Mexican legislative proposals and projects for Mexican borderlands development and industrialization are available. U.S. private enterprise would be well advised to scrutinize these legislative efforts in order to promote McAllen SMSA/Reynosa business cooperation and profitable symbiotic regional development. For example, the Mexican maquiladora program for borderland development, undertaken by the Secretaria de Patrimonio y Fomento Industrial, has become the best-known Mexican initiative for the promotion of regional industrial development in the borderlands.

Data Availability

Field observations on the availability of socioeconomic and business data are closely related to the implicit or explicit objectives of the established data sources discussed above. The researcher was impressed by the uncoordinated, or nonexistent, efforts in data compilation to develop and monitor business activities for industrial development in the McAllen/Reynosa borderlands. Data retrieval and publishing efforts were found to rely entirely on the initiatives of the private sector service agencies visited. The nature and categories of business data collected obviously depended on the particular criteria of prevailing office policies, and frequently appeared to be inconsistent over time. In one agency, for example, the researcher found that certain business statistics that had appeared in the references of a published article had been "thrown away" by a new administrator, destroying valuable evidence of industrial development. Apparent informality in data compilation appears to be a serious impediment to data availability.

The Mexican private sector was not found to be represented by private service agencies which actively promoted an exchange of business-related information. That is, the researcher found no evidence of such ongoing activities as business data collection and publication in the private sector service organizations contacted. There may be two reasons for this absence. In Mexico, the private industrial business sector has traditionally refrained from making business information and data public in an attempt to protect its monopolistic market advantages. Secondly, because of the increasing participation of the national government in the Mexican economy in both the productive and market sectors, the collection and publication of vital socioeconomic data have apparently been left to the corresponding Mexican authorities.

In the study of the industrial activities in the Reynosa borderlands, the scarcity of statistical data from the Mexican petroleum monopoly PEMEX is another factor which prevents the co-variate data presented in tables 1 through 4 from being complete. Approximately 14% of the gainfully employed population of Reynosa worked in the large PEMEX installations in the Reynosa borderlands during 1975. Statistics of this large industrial complex are not listed in the Mexican Census of Manufacturers. This notwithstanding, co-variate analysis of industrial, regional development, adjusted to include the PEMEX industrial statistics, will show an increased growth rate of the co-variate figures of Reynosa with respect to the McAllen SMSA.

---

[5] A maquiladora is a Mexican industrial manufacturing facility which produces economic goods with temporarily imported materials, for re-export (generally to the U.S. market). This type of Mexican industrial activity has been authorized by the Mexican government to permit foreign producers to use low-cost Mexican labor, and thus create jobs on the Mexican side of the border. The term maquiladora is often used in conjunction with the "twin-plant" concept, even though in the strict sense it represents a different type of industrial business arrangement.

Data Timeliness

In the survey of socioeconomic and business-related data to be applied for co-variate analysis of industrial technology transfer for regional development, ten statistics were identified (see table 1301). The data had been extracted from Mexican and U.S. census sources for 1970 and 1975. It was noted that private sector socioeconomic data collections depend heavily upon government sources. This is true for both the Mexican and U.S. private sectors. Undoubtedly, the importance of government-sponsored socioeconomic information is evident.

A major problem appears in a comparison of U.S. and Mexican census data. National census data collection presents a formidable task in both countries, involving the efforts of a large, national organization to organize, collect, review, and publish the compiled census data. As a result, there is a time lag of two to three years until census data are published in their final form. The field research was conducted in 1982, but the only complete census data available for the United States and Mexico were for 1970 and 1975. Between 1976 and 1981, however, Mexico enjoyed an unprecedented economic growth rate with a spectacular increase in the industrial base of the country. At the time of the field research, no statistical information on the increase in the economic development of the McAllen SMSA/Reynosa region was available. The research results, therefore, have to be taken as a conservative evaluation of co-variate analysis of regional development of the McAllen/Reynosa borderlands.

The Need for a Common Data Base

U.S.–Mexican borderlands studies to promote regional development will undoubtedly experience a considerable increase during the remainder of this decade. The borderlands economy, which is comprised of important and growing population concentrations on both sides of the border, their symbiotic interrelationships, and demands for attention and recognition for socioeconomic well-being, will capture the attention of regional and national policy makers. Some of the more visible borderlands issues are socioeconomic conditions; appropriate technologies; finance; industrialization; commerce; education; immigration; and tourism. Research on this unique regional economy will continue to focus on these and similar issues, and the resulting insights and recommendations will contribute to improved socioeconomic conditions in this binational area.

The research reported here emphasized field investigation to evaluate symbiotic interrelationships and regional development through industrial technology transfer in the McAllen/Reynosa region. A reliable data base for in-depth research and for the formulation of meaningful conclusions in the study of border issues was seen as indispensable. Deficiencies in sources, availability, and timeliness of data were discussed. Apparently uncoordinated data collection by public and private sector agencies in the U.S.–Mexican border region result in socioeconomic and business data which are frequently not comparable across the border. Instead of assisting researchers, the lack of data standardization tends to hinder and discourage scientific investigation.

The spectrum of data requirements and information flow for borderlands research presents a formidable problem of logistics. Classification of major issues, cataloging of information, and time series requirements are part of common data computerization. Coordinating activities, probably centralized in representative academic institutions throughout the borderlands, are expected to ensure the establishment of a common data base. The establishment of clearinghouses on both sides of the border constitutes an important step toward a workable organization for researchers of borderlands issues.

The field research has shown that the different socioeconomic, cultural, and political realities in Mexico and the United States have to be interpreted in their corresponding context before data from both independent national entities can be compared. Considerable organizational efforts will probably have to be made, and political hurdles must be crossed. However, inaction by the academic community and political representation of the area will only retard the indispensable requirement of a common data base for successful comparative borderlands research. Public- and private-sector policymakers on both sides of the border will be best served through academic support, evidenced by reliable U.S.–Mexican borderlands studies such as those mentioned here, in order to promote the accelerated development of the borderlands economy.

APPENDIX A

Summary of Data Sources: McAllen and Lower Rio Grande Valley of Texas

Federal Sources

1980 Census of Population, Volume 1, Chapter B. *General Population Characteristics, Part 45, Texas*. U.S. Department of Commerce, Bureau of the Census. U.S. Government Printing Office, Washington, D.C., August 1982.

1977 Census of Manufacturers, Geographic Area Series. *Texas*. U.S. Department of Commerce, Bureau of the Census. U.S. Government Printing Office, Washington, D.C., October 1980.

State Sources

Texas Employment Commission. *Texas Labor Market Reviews*. Austin, Texas, January–December 1982.

Texas 2000 Project, Office of the Governor. *Texas 2000 Commission Reports and Recommendations*. Austin, Texas, March 1982.

Texas 2000 Project, Office of the Governor. *Texas Past and Future: A Survey*. Austin, Texas, June 1981.

Texas Industrial Commission. *Investing Texas: A Guide for Foreign Manufacturers*. Austin, Texas, October 1980.

Private Sector Sources

McAllen Industrial Board. *Directory of Manufacturers, Fabricators*. McAllen, Texas, May 1982.

Rio Grande Valley Chamber of Commerce. *Statistical Data Book of the Rio Grande Valley of Texas*. Weslaco, Texas, 1982.

McAllen Chamber of Commerce. *McAllen, 1982–1983 Economic Facts and Figures*. McAllen, Texas, 1982.

Rio Grande Valley Chamber of Commerce. *Directory of Manufacturers in the Rio Grande Valley of Texas*. Weslaco, Texas, 1982.

Rio Grande Valley Chamber of Commerce. *Information about Industrial Opportunities in the Rio Grande Valley of Texas*. Weslaco, Texas, 1981.

Annual Report, Foreign-Trade Zone No. 12. *McAllen, Texas October 1, 1979–September 30, 1980*. McAllen, Texas, April 1981.

Institute for International Trade. *Border Business Indicators, Vol. 1, September 1, 1979–August 30, 1980*. Laredo State University, 1981.

Bureau of Business and Economic Research, School of Business Administration. *A Continuing Study of New McAllen Residents*. Pan American University, Edinburg, Texas, January 1980.

Burghardt, John A. Research Report 1978-3. *Major Trends in Population Growth in Texas*. Bureau of Business Research, University of Texas at Austin, Austin, Texas, November 1978.

APPENDIX B

Statistical Data Book of the Rio Grande Valley of Texas, Rio Grande Valley Chamber of Commerce, Weslaco, Texas, 1982 (76 pages)

Contents

Section 1: Introduction
- Map of the Rio Grande Valley
- County Maps and Basic County Information
  - Cameron County and South Padre Island Area
  - Hidalgo County
  - Starr County
  - Willacy County and Port Mansfield Area
- Valley History
- Valley Legislators
- Valley Weather

Section 2: Population
- Overview of Population, Economic Business Indicators, Retail Sales, Utility Connections, Bank Deposits
- Growth Information . . . to 2000
- Population of Major Cities, 1940–Current (1981)
- Ethnic Background of Current Population
- Population of All Cities and Towns
- Population Growth by Counties, 1950–1980
- Population Growth of Cities, 1900–1980
- Labor Force by Industries and Counties
- Vehicle Registration and Utilities Statistics
- 1980 Census Information as It Becomes Available

Section 3: Financial
- Ad Valoreni Tax Rates of Major Cities
- Effective Buying Power, Valley Counties 1940–Current
- Effective Buying Income per Household by Counties
- Retail Sales by Counties
- Sales Tax Refunds by Cities
- List of Area Banks and Savings and Loan Institutions

Bank Deposits, 1938–Current
December Business Barometers, 1942–latest December
Ten Years of Economic Growth

Section 4: Agriculture and Industry
Overview and Summary of Agricultural Crops
Irrigation Survey Summary Showing Irrigated Acreage
Farm Cash Income, 1924–Current
Farm Cash Income by Commodity for Year, 1972–Current
Cotton Production by Counties, 1920–Current
Citrus Production by Year

Other Industries
Mineral Income by Counties
Shrimp Landings in Valley Ports
Other Production Information

Section 5: Tourism
General Information
Variety of Tourists
Texas Department of Highways and Public Transportation, Visitor Estimates
Estimated Annual Income from Tourism
Bridge Crossings to Mexico
Progreso-Nuevo Progreso
Brownsville-Matamoros
McAllen-Hidalgo-Reynosa

APPENDIX C

Summary of Data Sources: Reynosa, Tamaulipas, Mexico

Federal Sources

Gobierno del Estado de Tamaulipas, Secretaría de Fomento Económico y Turismo, Dirección de Análisis y Proyectos. *Información básica municipal, Reynosa*. Tamaulipas, March, 1982.

Dirección General de Promoción Fiscal CEPROFI, Secretaría de Hacienda y Crédito Público. *Nuevos estímulos fiscales*. México, D.F., 1982.

Coordinación General del Programa Nacional de Desarrollo de Franjas Fronterizas y Zona Libres. *Los programas de desarrollo de las fronteras y zonas libres y la CODEF*. México, D.F., 1981.

Secretaría de Patrimonio y Fomento Industrial, Dirección General de Industrias. *México—: qué es una maquiladora?* México, D.F., 1981.

Secretaría de Programación y Presupuesto, Coordinación General del Sistema Nacional de Información. *X Censo Industrial 1976*. Datos de 1975, Resumen General, Tomo I. México, D.F., 1979.

Estados Unidos Mexicanos, Secretaría de Industria y Comercio, Dirección General de Estadística. *IX Censo Industrial 1971*. Tomo I, Resumen General. México, D.F., 1973.

Regional Private Sector Agencies

Emilio Martínez Manatou, Candidato a la Gubernatura del Estado de Tamaulipas. *Reynosa*. (Monografia). Reynosa, Tamaulipas, 1979.

Planeación Arquitectónica, PLAR, S.C., Ciudad Industrial de Reynosa, Tamaulipas. *Estudio socioeconómico y análisis de mercado*. México, D.F., September, 1979.

14

United States—Mexico Border Economic Interdependence: Input-Output Model Perspectives of the Effects of the 1982 Peso Devaluations on the San Diego Economy

Kenneth L. Shellhammer

In 1978 a research team at San Diego State University began a project designed to link urban areas of the California border with urban areas of Baja California through an interindustry (input-output) framework. The project was connected a year later with a parallel effort by the Centro Nacional de Información y Estadísticas del Trabajo (CENIET) of the Mexican Ministry of Labor. To date, the products of that research consist of: (1) a survey-based input-out model of San Diego;[1] (2) a survey-based input-output model of Imperial Valley;[2] and (3) a survey-based matrix of technical coefficients for the state of Baja California. The first two products were completed by the California Border Area Resource Center at San Diego State University under grants from the U.S. Department of Housing and Urban Development and the Ford Foundation (New York). The third was a joint effort by a number of government agencies in Mexico, including CENIET.

Much can be learned from the models that currently exist. By way of demonstrating the potential of the models for the purpose of this paper, we have produced what we regard as a "conservative plausible" scenario of what happened to San Diego/Mexico border transactions in 1982. Then, using the San Diego input-output model, we estimate the economic impact of that scenario.

Scenario Rationale

During the period from 1978 (the base year for the survey of transactions from which the CBARC input-output model was estimated) to 1982 (the year when the peso was extensively devalued relative to the dollar), the following economic changes occurred:

General price inflation in both countries, more so in Mexico than in the United States.

Rapid real economic growth in both countries, but much more so in Mexico than in the United States.

Overevaluation of the Mexican peso relative to the U.S. dollar.

All three changes led to increasing demand by Mexicans for U.S. products—particularly in the "Free Zone"

---

[1]Norris C. Clement and Kenneth L. Shellhammer, "The CBARC Input-Output Model of San Diego," California Border Area Resource Center, San Diego State University, San Diego, California, 1981.
[2]Clement and Shellhammer, "The CBARC Input-Output Model of imperial Valley," California Border Area Resource Center, San Diego State University, San Diego, California, 1981.

area of Baja California, which is relatively unencumbered by trade restrictions. Therefore, we assume that rate of growth of purchases by Mexicans in the city of San Diego increased in *real* terms at an annual rate of 10%. Applying this rate of increase to the survey-based estimates of transactions with Mexico results in estimates of direct sales to Mexico by San Diego industries, shown in column (1) of table 1400. These estimates represent what sales would have been (in thousands of 1982 dollars) had there been no devaluation.

Column (2) of table 1400 shows what we judge to be an equally conservative plausible scenario of estimates of differences between column (1) transactions and actual 1982 transactions, which we would call the initial direct effects of the 1982 devaluations of the peso. Column (2) estimates are based upon a 50% reduction in consumer goods and services (primarily Tijuana consumers), which were the transactions primarily curtailed in the immediate months following the initial devaluation.

The estimates in column (3) of are 50% reductions across the board from column (1) transactions. These include all trade in intermediate goods and services and investment goods and services, in addition to the 50% reduction in consumer purchases. This, we would suggest, is a plausible scenario of the current state of affairs, which is likely to continue through the balance of 1983.

Economic Impacts

Using the CBARC input-output model of San Diego, we have estimated the direct, indirect, and induced effects on output, income, and employment in San Diego resulting from the transactions with Mexico specified in table 1400. The results of these simulations are shown in tables 1401–1403. Table 1401 is the baseline estimate of the economic impact in San Diego of trade with Mexico in 1982, had there been no devaluation. The baseline estimates in table 1401 show overall transactions in San Diego attributable to trade (potential) with Mexico in 1982 at $1.4 billion. This figure includes the $.4 billion of personal income received by San Diego households, but excludes any merchandise exports through the Port of San Diego that bypassed San Diego businesses. It also excludes approximately $.6 billion of resale merchandise imported to San Diego for export to Mexico, passing through San Diego's wholesale and retail trade sectors.

Table 1402 shows the direct, indirect, and induced reductions in San Diego output, income, and employment attributable to the estimated reductions in consumer goods

Table 1400

ESTIMATED TRADE AND CHANGES IN TRADE BETWEEN MEXICO AND SAN DIEGO, 1982

(T US)

Sector	Direct Changes		
	Scenario 1	Scenario 2	Scenario 3
Agriculture	17,368	~	−8,685
Livestock/Products	8,275	~	−4,138
Fishing	1,954	~	−977
Mining/Petroleum Products	977	~	−488
Manufacturers/Food and Products	4,491	~	−2,246
Manufacturers/Textile Products	4,585	~	−2,293
Manufacturers/Wood/Paper Products	19,833	~	−9,916
Printing/Publishing	8,519	~	−4,261
Manufacturers/Chemicals and Products	238	~	−119
Manufacturers/Metal and Products	3,900	~	−1,950
Manufacturers/Machinery	168,435	~	−84,219
Manufacturers/Transportation Equipment	2,807	~	−1,404
All Other Manufacturers	13,036	~	−6,519
Residential Construction	581	~	−292
Other Construction	7,074	~	−3,537
Electricity/Gas/Sanitary	25,423	~	−12,712
Transportation	16,975	~	−8,488
Communications	~	~	0
Wholesale Trade	136,356	−68,178	−68,178
Retail Grocery Stores	31,115	−15,558	−15,558
Other Retail Stores	101,140	−50,571	−50,571
Hotel/Motel/Restaurant	40,500	−20,250	0
Financial/Insurance/Real Estate	7,639	~	−3,820
Business Services	86	~	−42
Other Services	50,437	−25,218	−25,218
Households	~	~	~
Total	671,746	−179,775	−315,630

SOURCE: CDARC–San Diego Economic Impact Model.

and services trade. The negative $.4 billion in overall transactions includes $127 million in personal income but excludes reductions in pass-through transactions of at least $300 million. The impacts shown in table 1402 are probably reasonable approximations of the impact of the devaluation on the San Deigo economy in 1982.

Table 1403 shows the direct, indirect, and induced effects based upon the third scenario in table 1400. This extends the 50% reduction to all goods and services trade, including investment goods and intermediate goods. This scenario of negative change is probably larger than that actually experienced in 1982 because it takes longer for an adjustment in these types of economic relations. Nevertheless, we would suggest that the impacts shown in table 1403 are probably viable estimates of the 1983 impacts.

Summary and Conclusions

This essay has presented what should only be regarded as crude estimates of the economic impact of the Mexican peso devaluation on the economy of San Diego. Anyone interested in greater precision should examine a number of sources, including customs information, retail sales data, and localized shopping and unemployment data. Nevertheless, we would argue that the items not covered in this analysis are likely to introduce larger errors of estimation than those contained in any analysis of the direct trade effects.

We did not estimate the impact of San Diegans shifting from San Diego stores to Tijuana stores to take advantage of post-devaluation bargains. Nor could we analyze the overall feedback effects of these shifts on the economies of San Diego and Tijuana. These effects could be as large as those that were covered here. Also, in the larger scheme of things, the border transaction effects represent the mechanism of Mexico's effort to recover from the crises: the redirection of dollars out of the borderlands and into debt finance and refinance. In this regard, we can be sure that until the Mexican economy's export base is firmed up, the stopgap measures will weigh heavily on both sides of the U.S.-Mexico border economies.

What is learned from the analysis is that the San

Development of Data

Table 1401

DIRECT, INDIRECT, AND INDUCED EFFECTS OF TRADE BETWEEN MEXICO AND SAN DIEGO, 1982, BASELINE ESTIMATES (NO DEVALUATION)

Sector	Output T US	Output %	Income T US	Income %	Employment Actual	Employment %	Sector (%)
Agriculture	21,076	1.49	8,349	2.07	657	3.69	4.29
Livestock/Products	10,750	.76	3,457	.86	97	.54	8.38
Fishing	3,786	.27	1,347	.33	51	.28	3.90
Mining/Petroleum Products	1,926	.14	708	.18	17	.09	2.52
Manufacturers/Food and Products	8,797	.62	1,571	.39	53	.30	.85
Manufacturers/Textile Products	5,066	.36	1,147	.28	162	.91	3.97
Manufacturers/Wood/Paper Products	22,448	1.59	7,114	1.77	344	1.93	12.72
Printing/Publishing	14,250	1.01	3,940	.98	172	.96	2.98
Manufacturers/Chemicals and Products	1,015	.07	149	.04	5	.03	.33
Manufacturers/Metal and Products	8,250	.58	2,469	.61	101	.57	1.72
Manufacturers/Machinery	172,519	12.19	59,593	14.79	2,071	11.64	7.34
Manufacturers/Transportation Equipment	3,835	.27	1,395	.35	50	.28	.19
All Other Manufacturers	17,941	1.27	4,612	1.14	219	1.23	1.97
Residential Construction	4,065	.29	460	.11	15	.09	.14
Other Construction	16,888	1.19	4,610	1.14	189	1.06	.55
Electricity/Gas/Sanitary	55,712	3.94	12,826	3.18	282	1.58	4.54
Transportation	27,985	1.98	8,149	2.02	366	2.06	3.44
Communications	16,945	1.20	5,695	1.41	197	1.11	1.90
Wholesale Trade	158,318	11.18	78,708	19.53	2,721	15.29	12.35
Retail Grocery Stores	41,162	2.91	18,089	3.25	1,202	6.76	7.34
Other Retail Stores	136,748	9.66	68,630	17.03	3,780	21.24	5.74
Hotel/Motel/Restaurant	59,938	4.23	16,124	4.00	1,992	11.20	3.75
Finance/Insurance/Real Estate	87,190	6.16	46,545	11.55	699	3.93	1.98
Business Services	15,294	1.08	4,362	1.08	271	1.52	1.16
Other Services	100,662	7.11	47,901	11.89	2,081	11.70	2.18
Households	402,950	28.47	~	~	~	~	1.86
Total	1,415,516	100.00	402,950	100.00	17,793	100.00	
Percentage of Region Total		2.55		3.35		2.25	2.55

SOURCE: CBARC–San Diego Economic Impact Model.

Diego economy, overall, may not notice the effects of its role in Mexico's economic crises. Certainly, those people who were most directly dependent on Mexican markets will know. However, the substantial growth that took place in the Mexico connection between 1978 and 1982, translated to a percentage of San Diego economic activity, represents a growth of from 1.66% to 3.35%, and the devaluation represents a decrease of at most −1.6%. This effect may be large enough for San Diego to lag slightly in the recovery from the 1981–1982 recession. But most discussions of the change in San Diego unemployment statistics compared to changes in the United States do not discuss the Mexico problem. This is unfortunate for the thousands of San Diegans whose economic opportunities rise and fall with the border economy. Although in absolute amounts, the devaluation impact in San Diego was probably greater than in any border city (with the possible exception of El Paso, Texas), in relative terms it could account for only a small fraction of the unemployment rate in San Diego. Imperial County, California, which has much smaller direct trade with Mexico, experienced an increase in unemployment of almost 10% in 1982. Unemployment there is currently around 30%, making it one of the most depressed counties in the United States.

It is very difficult to define appropriate policies for economic problems and opportunities in the absence of economic models that cross the border. I have been able to draw some conclusions from current events, but only because I had the benefit of a model designed to be binational. The model still falls far short of being able to analyze the San Diego/Tijuana economic region as a partially integrated economic system in the context of two independent national economies. As we work further with the three models mentioned, we may learn more about the nature of the borderlands economy and methods of modeling the interdependence of the two neighboring nations.

Table 1402

ECONOMIC IMPACT OF THE MEXICAN PESO DEVALUATION ON SAN DIEGO, 1982, LOW-RANGE ESTIMATES (WITH DEVALUATION)

TYPE II IMPACTS: DIRECT, INDIRECT, AND INDUCED EFFECTS

Sector	Output T US	Output %	Income T US	Income %	Employment Actual	Employment %	Sector (%)
Agriculture	−1,104	.26	−437	.34	−31	.52	−.22
Livestock/Products	−800	.19	−257	.20	−7	.11	−.62
Fishing	−533	.13	−190	.15	−7	.11	−.55
Mining/Petroleum Products	−189	.05	−70	.05	−2	.03	−.25
Manufacturers/Food and Products	−1,067	.26	−190	.15	−6	.10	−.10
Manufacturers/Textile Products	−148	.04	−33	.03	−4	.06	−.12
Manufacturers/Wood/Paper Products	−623	.15	−197	.16	−9	.15	−.35
Printing/Publishing	−1,634	.39	−452	.36	−20	.34	−.34
Manufacturers/Chemicals and Products	−148	.04	−22	.02	−1	.01	−.05
Manufacturers/Metal and Products	−337	.08	−101	.08	−4	.07	−.07
Manufacturers/Machinery	−436	.10	−151	.12	−6	.10	−.02
Manufacturers/Transportation Equipment	−216	.05	−79	.06	−3	.05	−.01
All Other Manufacturers	−461	.11	−119	.09	−5	.09	−.05
Residential Construction	−1,061	.25	−120	.09	−4	.07	−.04
Other Construction	−2,118	.51	−578	.45	−27	.44	−.07
Electricity/Gas/Sanitary	−10,035	2.40	−2,310	1.82	−52	.88	−.82
Transportation	−3,694	.88	−1,076	.85	−48	.80	−.45
Communications	−5,907	1.41	−1,985	1.56	−69	1.16	−.66
Wholesale Trade	−75,365	18.05	−37,468	29.44	−1,302	21.84	−5.88
Retail Grocery Stores	−18,730	4.49	−5,956	4.68	−546	9.16	−3.34
Other Retail Stores	−62,005	14.85	−31,188	24.45	−1,711	28.70	−2.60
Hotel/Motel/Restaurant	−26,453	6.34	−7,116	5.59	−878	14.73	−1.66
Finance/Insurance/Real Estate	−28,363	6.79	−15,141	11.90	−231	3.87	−.64
Business Services	−5,831	1.40	−1,663	1.31	−103	1.72	−.44
Other Services	−42,955	10.29	−20,441	16.06	−883	14.89	−.93
Households	−127,270	30.48	~	~	~	~	−.59
Total	−417,483	100.00	−127,270	100.00	−5,964	100.00	
Percentage of Region Total	−.75		−1.06		−.75		−.75

SOURCE: CBARC San Diego Economic Impact Model.

Table 1403

ECONOMIC IMPACT OF THE MEXICAN PESO DEVALUATION ON SAN DIEGO, 1982, HIGH-RANGE ESTIMATES (WITH DEVALUATION)

TYPE II IMPACTS: DIRECT, INDIRECT, AND INDUCED EFFECTS

Sector	Output T US	Output %	Income T US	Income %	Employment Actual	Employment %	Sector (%)
Agriculture	−10,297	1.54	−4,079	2.12	−322	3.98	−2.10
Livestock/Products	−5,096	.76	−1,639	.85	−46	.57	−3.97
Fishing	−1,669	.25	−594	.31	−23	.28	−1.72
Mining/Petroleum Products	−949	.14	−349	.18	−8	.10	−1.24
Manufacturers/Food and Products	−3,992	.60	−713	.37	−24	.30	−.38
Manufacturers/Textile Products	−2,505	.37	−567	.30	−80	.99	−1.96
Manufacturers/Wood/Paper Products	−11,177	1.67	−3,542	1.84	−171	2.11	−6.33
Printing/Publishing	−6,857	1.03	−1,896	.99	−83	1.02	−1.44
Manufacturers/Chemicals and Products	−459	.07	−67	.03	−3	.03	−.15
Manufacturers/Metal and Products	−4,080	.61	−1,221	.64	−50	.62	−.85
Manufacturers/Machinery	−86,222	12.90	−29,783	15.49	−1,035	12.79	−3.67
Manufacturers/Transportation Equipment	−1,884	.28	−685	.36	−25	.30	−.09
All Other Manufacturers	−8,925	1.33	−2,294	1.19	−109	1.35	−.98
Residential Construction	−1,972	.29	−223	.12	−8	.09	−.07
Other Construction	−8,270	1.24	−2,258	1.17	−92	1.14	−.27
Electricity/Gas/Sanitary	−26,731	4.00	−6,154	3.20	−135	1.67	−2.18
Transportation	−13,688	2.05	−3,986	2.07	−179	2.21	−1.68
Communications	−8,032	1.20	−2,700	1.40	−93	1.15	−.90
Wholesale Trade	−78,410	11.73	−38,982	20.28	−1,350	16.67	−6.12
Retail Grocery Stores	−20,349	3.04	−6.471	3.37	−595	7.35	−3.63
Other Retail Stores	−67,568	10.11	−33,910	17.64	−1,868	23.08	−2.84
Hotel/Motel/Restaurant	−9,215	1.38	−2,479	1.29	−318	3.93	−.58
Finance/Insurance/Real Estate	−41,776	6.25	−22,301	11.60	−336	4.15	−.95
Business Services	−7,291	1.09	−2,079	1.08	−129	1.60	−.55
Other Services	−48,940	7.32	−23,289	12.11	−1,013	12.51	−1.06
Households	−192,262	28.76	∼	∼	∼	∼	−.89
Total	−668,616	100.00	−192,262	100.00	−8,094	100.00	
Percentage of Region Total	−1.21		−1.60		−1.02		−1.21

SOURCE: CBARC–San Diego Economic Impact Model.

Contributors

Mike Farrell, a graduate of Pomona College and Stanford University, has been a member of the economics faculty at California State University, Long Beach since 1969. His continuing interest in the problems of trade and development in Latin America stems from a 1966 Ford Foundation grant to study the impact of trade restrictions on the development of the Chilean textile industry. In 1973–1974 he lectured at the Universidad Nacional de San Agustín in Arequipa, Peru, as a Fulbright Scholar. The research for this chapter was performed while on sabbatical leave from the State University System.

Jerry R. Ladman holds the Ph.D. in economics from Iowa State University. He has been working on Mexican projects since 1965 when he began his dissertation research in that country. He has lived in Mexico for some three years, holding appointments in program management for the Mexico City office of the Ford Foundation and as a visiting professor in the Graduate College of the National Agricultural University in Chapingo. His published research has dealt with Mexican agriculture—especially credit, internal migration, foreign trade, tourism, border assembly plants, the twin-city border economy, and the economic history of the Mexicali Valley. He is co-editor of *United States–Mexican Energy Relations*.

Peter L. Reich, editor of this volume, is a doctoral candidate in history at UCLA and a second-year law student at UC Berkeley. He has been a Chancellor's Intern Fellow at UCLA, and has held Fulbright, Social Science Research Council, and NDEA Title VI fellowships for research in Mexico. Co-editor for three volumes of the *Statistical Abstract of Latin America* (1977, 1978, and 1980), Reich has published widely on the application of quantitative methods to Latin American studies. Reich's current research, including his dissertation, focuses on modern Mexican legal history and church-state relations.

Martin E. Rosenfeldt is Associate Professor of Management at North Texas State University. He holds a Ph.D. in business administration and degrees in industrial and mechanical engineering. He has extensive international management and consulting experience in private business. Rosenfeldt has held academic appointments at the Instituto Tecnológico y de Estudios Superiores de Monterrey and at the Universidad Autónoma de Nuevo León, Mexico.

Juan Salcedo, research assistant for this volume, received his B.A. in history from Stanford University (1980) and his M.B.A. in finance/accounting from UCLA (1983). He is currently an auditor for the accounting firm of Deloitte, Haskins and Sells in Los Angeles, and maintains an interest in Mexico-United States financial relations.

Kenneth L. Shellhammer is an Adjunct Professor of Economics at San Diego State University. He is also Senior Economist at Regional Economic Research in San Diego and a Ford Foundation Fellow at the Centro de Estudios Fronterizos del Norte de México, Tijuana, B.C. He received his Ph.D. in economics from the University of Colorado and has extensive experience in the construction and application of input-output models at regional levels.